WHAT TO EXPECT IN THIS BOOK:

* *tentacle sex*

* *Kathy Acker*

* *the violent deaths of male genius artists, philosophers and theorists*

* *zombies*

* *sirens*

* *biohacking*

* *rampant plagiarism*

* *cop killing*

* *spells you can use at home*

VIRUS

LINDA STUPART

AM

Arcadia Missa Publications

Unit 6 Bellenden Business Centre
Bellenden Road
Peckham
London SE15 4RF

www.arcadiamissa.com
@ArcadiaMissa
info@arcadiamissa.com

VIRUS, 2016

Cover artwork by Linda Stupart
Illustrations by Linda, Tom, Tia and Isla
Design by Zhoe Granger

ISBN: 978-0-9926747-8-6

With additional editing by Ray Filar & Arcadia Missa.

LOTTERY FUNDED

Arcadia Missa Publications are available from the gallery, our website and selected stockists.

DWELLERS IN THE REALM OF THE LIVING DEAD

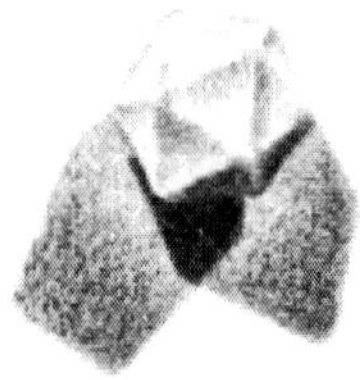

VIRUS

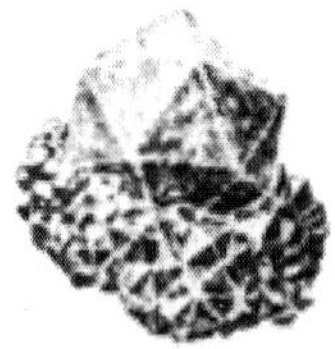

PYRITE CRYSTAL

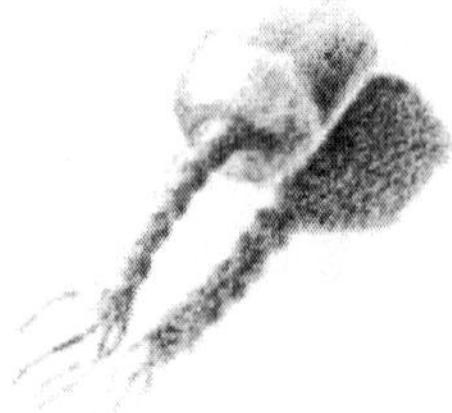

VIRUS

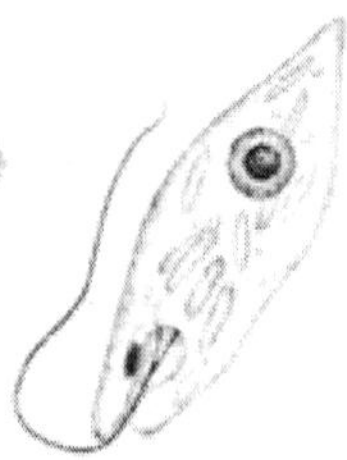

EUGLENA

NEITHER FISH NOR FOWL

Until the discovery of the virus, scientists felt that even if life was difficult to define they could at least distinguish between animate and inanimate matter. But the virus cannot accurately be described as either. Some are shaped very much like pyrite or other mineral crystals; others resemble living organisms such as the euglena. The virus has no means of locomotion, it possesses no source of power and it cannot grow. On the other hand, a virus contains vital DNA or RNA; like living matter, it can reproduce but not until it has commandeered a cell. It can reduce a healthy, productive cell to a mere nursery that fosters a new generation of viruses.

I want to show you a body.

They are sitting on a rock that is covered in moss. The body is holding a knife and wearing Doc Martens with flowers on the sides and they are whittling something out of dead wood. They are whittling a 3d model of a pulsating blob GIF out of dead wood. It has too many dimensions, and so they are struggling to get it right.

As the knife separates the layers of woodskin they are softly chanting the word "caress," because this is the future, and the word has become a war cry, or a weapon.
The knife slips and cuts a minuscule chip out of the brown wood and of their brown thumb. They are smiling and they are bleeding all over it.

There is a body and they are sitting on a rock. Let them narrate this story for you, this story of the future.

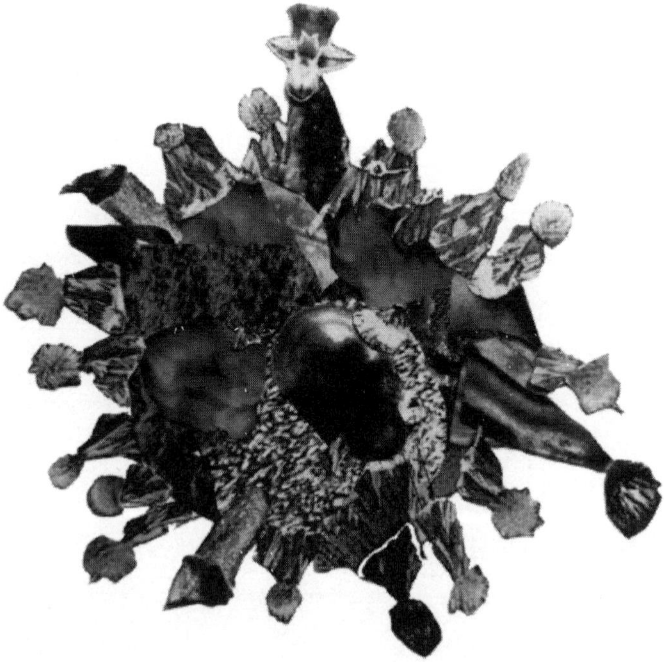

Prelude (1985): A death drop/after the fall. Once upon a time there was a shadow, or a silhouette; silueta - *they carve a shadow out of wood, the cut scabbed over but always threatening to open up* – once upon a time there was a shadow and her name was Ana Mendieta.

Men were angry because this shadow appeared to become real before their eyes; to enter language and also art galleries. Men became angry because this shadow grew a body from the mud and trees and the cow's heart it swallowed. Men became angry because the shadow became naked became a woman became a name, became Ana Mendieta and so she dropped, she fell.

After Ana Mendieta fell from the window of the apartment almost all of the bones in her almost naked body were shattered. After she fell from the window of the 34th floor apartment all of her major organs were split open. After she fell from the window of the 34th floor apartment on Mercer her body was never photographed, which is strange since that was her practice. After she fell

269 feet from the window of the 34th floor apartment on Mercer a male pathologist dictated to stenographer Dorothy Stevens that her body was white, which is strange because brownness and skin were her practice. After she fell 269 feet from the window of the 34th floor apartment on Mercer in 4.21 seconds the male pathologist cut open her chest and took out her heart and weighed it; this was also her practice.

There is a body and they are sitting on a rock and they are telling this story. In the future there is a body and they want to tell a story of the decay of figure into ground, larvae playing under skin shining many eyed flies popping stitches in her chest alive malevolent snakes churning open mouthed waiting for revenge in the earth beneath the still performing silueta. But after she fell 269 feet from the window of the 34th floor Minimalist apartment on Mercer in 4.21 seconds, what remained of Ana Mendieta's body was cremated.

After she fell 269 feet from the window of the 34th floor Minimalist apartment on Mercer in 4.21 seconds at a velocity of 120 miles per hour male artist Carl Andre, her husband of only eight months, suggested that she might have suicided because he was more famous than her, which is strange because he had fresh scratches on his nose and forearms and because people had heard her screaming and because she had called friends to say she was scared of him and because she was so scared of heights and because he changed his story so many times and because he had left her before in 1983 because she refused to turn down the Prix de Rome in sculpture and its yearlong residency, which would have made her more famous than him, for a moment.

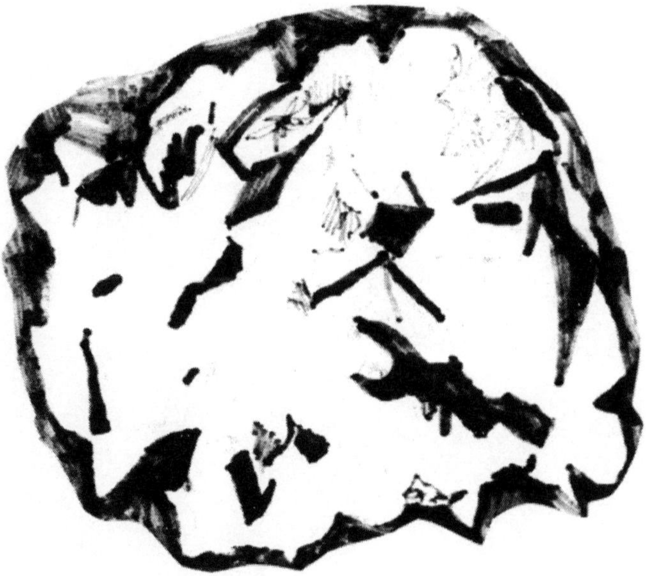

Some decades later and an American philosopher-explorer, Alphonso Lingis, is standing in front of a packed lecture theater. Panpipes are playing a simulation of world music and behind him there are huge projected photographs of black men and black women and a man has a spike through his nose.

By venturing literally from the First World to the Third World, Al Lingus has tried to reconnect human consciousness to his external reality. As a wanderer and a cosmopolitan philosopher, he is perpetually in search of sensations and constantly giving expression to the sensualities he encounters in exotic far away spaces. This sensuality is not only sought out in each of Lingis' travels: it operates as a condition of possibility in his philosophy.

Al Lingus speaks:

> I look out my window, past the curtain, my room a third floor apartment in Downtown New York and I see her, as she walks along the street. I cannot touch her... she cannot

touch me... we, do not touch each other. I do not know what she thinks, how she feels, her worries, her loves, her...losses. She cannot know what I think, as I watch her through the third floor window of my downtown apartment, my feeling, my yearning. No contact, no caress, no touch, no intimacy... and, if she were to mount the stairs to the third floor of my apartment, pass the threshold and walk into the room where I stand looking through the window, even then, even then, we would not touch, there could never be a true touch or understanding between us. Merely a cold caress.

I see many people walk along the street through the window of my third floor apartment in Downtown New York and yet we never touch, there can be no contact. I touch myself, I finger the cuff of the sleeve of my jacket where it hangs down creating a cavern below my arm... but it is no true touch. If another cannot touch me, cannot truly know me, can I ever touch myself? Sometimes, I walk down the stairs and onto the street below and I walk along the sidewalk. I brush those who I pass on the street... a soft caress, a momentary hint of intimacy but it only increases my sense of a lack of intimacy with its faint promise. If only I, in the third floor apartment could see me walk along the street, then perhaps there would be an impossible moment of contact, of a final knowledge, that which transcends carnality, the communion of the caress....

Behind him, projected men who he has photographed are dancing with skeletons painted on their skin, showing through their skin. A man with dirty feet and clear eyes is looking straight out at the camera. His lips are wet. He spits; a curse. And now the pale worm American philosopher-explorer Alphonso Lingis is losing colour. Veins show through his skin blue and wriggling. He is talking about contact, about touch, about the weight of the body about the moment of caressing language, caressing a body,

caressing

a

woman

who he sees under his window.

He is slowing down and his skin is leaching out. The warm dribble from the body above and behind him flows over his white thinning hair. Flows over The Body, gets caught in its wrinkles, rivulets in between its toes, its pale testes, under its dilapidated foreskin or translucent circumcision scar. The toxic saliva is eating at the flesh of Alphonso Lingus, the philosopher-explorer, who reinvents philosophy through his unique way of looking at the FAR AWAY COUNTRIES

He

Regularly explores.

Al Lingus the philosopher-explorer is starting to disappear on contact with the image he shot first.

The philosopher-explorer is degrading as skin begins to peel.

The audience backs away from the crumpled object, the dead man, the body. They retreat, mumbling, towards the back of the lecture theatre while the faux panpipes continue to make contact with the limp grey body of the philosopher-explorer, Al Lingus. The audience barely discerns the hum of the lecture theatre lights, the microphone, the static now-dead crackle. Their skin prickles with the air conditioning common to the university and the morgue. The audience attempts emancipation, and escapes via the fire exit.

After they leave they lock the door and slowly vines and ferns and alien trees begin to grow over the lecture theatre. The fluorescent light has been left on and its rays dapple across what is left of his now squirming skin.

Those who find ecstasy do so not by visiting the shrines of civilization but by trudging in the swamps of human destitution and misery.

This is the beginning of the virus.

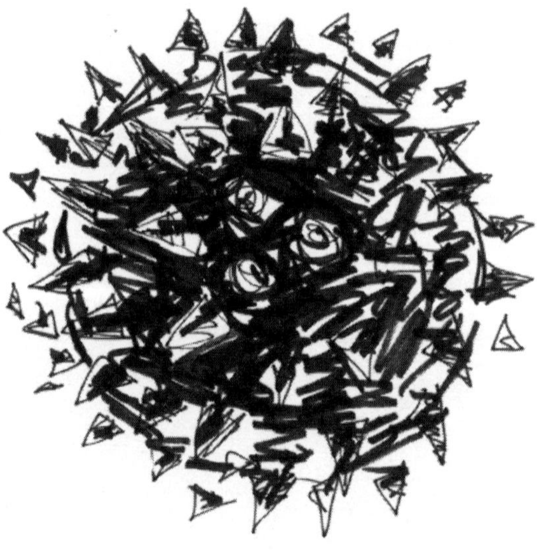

The virus is blue and has lumps shaped like rocks and it has tiny yellow dots and the dots are the virus. Virus is red and has a hundred tentacles and they cling to everything. Virus has a killer body. Virus is not alive: she does not have cells and she cannot turn food into energy and without a host she is an inert sac of chemicals and code. Virus is not dead: she has genes, she reproduces independently of any masculine force, she evolves. Virus is a small chip of software that rides on top of the backs of other programs that think they are real. Each time the program runs, virus runs too. She runs faster and she either reproduces through other programs, through other bodies, or causes chaosmutation inside her mount. Virus is a turquoise blue 3d model with legs that stick out everywhere and each leg has a ball at the end. The virus must inject her DNA helix into a cell inside a body. The viral DNA uses the cell's and the body's and the canon's existing machinery until it bursts in skin shreds, releasing the virus. In other cases the new virus particles bud off the cell one at a time and the cell body remains alive, though mutated.

Virus comes from the Latin word for "poison" or "slimy liquid". A worm is a small piece of software that uses computer networks and security holes to replicate itself. A copy of the worm scans the network for another. Virus doesn't die if she can't find a hoștbody, she just hibernates, lays dormant, and waits for the right conditions to come along so she can make copies of herself. These copies are identical to the first virus and usually so many are made the host cell explodes. The new viruses spread to the cells next door and then the cells next to these, infecting bodies of knowledge bit by bit. Just one virus in a body can make thousands of copies of itself and disable that body from within. In the past scientists suspected that a large DNA-based virus took up residence inside a bacterial cell more than a billion years ago to create the first cell nucleus. If so, then we are all descended from viruses.

But it wants to kill us.
- No, they want something.|- It wants to mutilate us|just like it did the other men.
Did you see the lecture theatre?|That thing wants something from us.
Why don't we talk to it ? It's in|the computer. We could talk to it.
- What ?|- Talk to it ! It's in the computer.
What the hell ?|What do I do ? What do I do ?
Please help me.|I need English, please.
"Who are you ?"
I am aware.

Is that it ? Is it ?|Is it the thing ?

"We mean you no harm."

Life-form analysis complete.|Species is de-structive,

invasive, noxious,|harmful to the body of the whole.

- "What species ?"|- Man.

You are virus.

Great. Just great.

It thinks we're germs.

"What do you want from us ?"

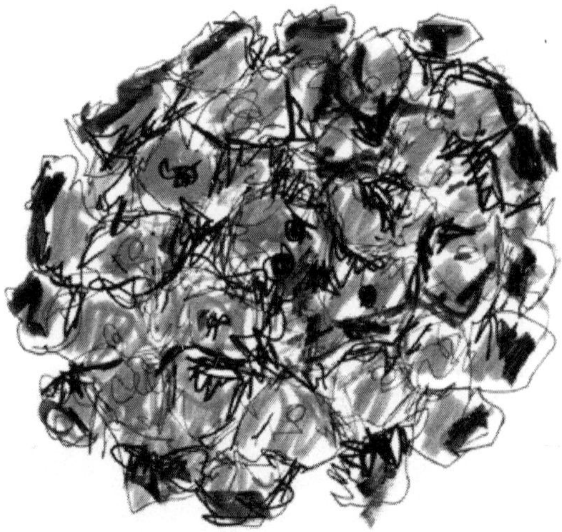

Before Virus started to spill out of the computer, oozing up through keyboards, escaping screens and webcams and the rays of projectors, she was bubbling inside of every piece of communication technology, but especially those in the service of the canon, the knowledge industries…

The virus' life is continual reproduction, and so she festers, feeds, multiplies in the technologies of Oedipal teleologies father fucking father killing daddy daddy oh daddy Oh! Oh! Oh! Every time a white man born a man cites a man born a man cites a man again every time a translucent male artist or academic or scientist references another pallid male academic, artist or scientist – in this most sterile shallow procreative model, she proliferates. In every screen, in every projector, ever lecture theatre hub, Virus was growing new tentacles, legs, cunts, arms with balls on the end like the viruses that used to be in science class when there were still classes and when they still insisted on believing in science, and objectivity - that is men's ability to make objects of the world.

In the past they had tried to tell them, warn them (worn thin). At every single conference or lecture around the world they'd say: HI HAVE YOU THOUGHT ABOUT HOW YOU'RE TALKING ABOUT THE FUTURE BUT YOU'VE ONLY CITED WHITE MEN HEY HOW ARE YOU GONNA STOP THAT HEY WHAT KIND OF FUTURE *IS* THAT?

But every body grows tired eventually, even this one. The same words again and again wearing out their throat their blood their muscles knotting, stomach filled with black oil, fingers tapping on the seat of every lecture theatre. But, no, nobody can say they didn't try to warn them.

After that day when the noble savage exited the image through the virus' forever multiplying maternal matrix; since then, every time a white man is quoted by a white man quoting a white man quoting a OR an Other is abjected/objected/thinged by a white man quoting a… that Other exits the images too, the texts; riding in on the pulsing breeding violent Virus whore.

Each time a white man born a man with a dick that is his voice, every time that dick imagines an-other, Virus jumps from the screen and then the page and then the word: enters veins. The virus is born of men on men in men in an ironic refusal of their heterosexual division of labour, but she is indiscriminate, she enters every body she can touch.

(Reproduction might be outside the body in the future, but that doesn't mean it's not still fucking dangerous.)

Not everybody died like philosopher-explorer Alphonso Lingus, though. Bodies quickly learned the way to survive the virus was to be violable, to be porous, to be *lacking in boundary integrity,* to be an old object, full of holes and able to die over and over again. People become forms: porous bodies exhaling microbes, spasmodically spreading deliriums, viruses, pollutions, toxins.

Those who were already used to it, already objectified, already abject, already broken, already dead; took this pretty easily. Not so the others. The murderers fell first.

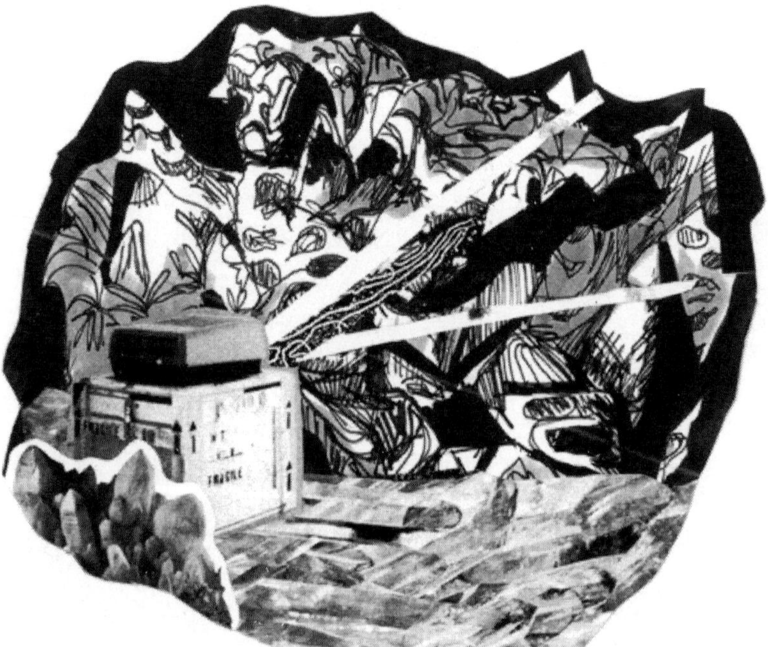
FRAGILE

A SPELL FOR BINDING ALL-MALE CONFERENCE PANELS

This spell could also be adjusted to bind the tongues of those sprouting hate speech while simultaneously claiming they are unable to speak

YOU WILL NEED:

Myrrh

A small piece of moss

A large piece of red felt

Black thread

A large empty jar with a lid or a Tupperware container

Scissors

Printouts of papers written by the men on the conference panel, preferably ones that only cite white men – you could also put these papers on a memory stick.

You might also want some rose or clear quartz to focus your energy and banish masculine authority

This spell should be spoken in a dark or full moon phase, and if possible on a Saturday

Ideally this spell should be performed in the lecture theatre or conference venue where the all male panel will be hosted. If not, any sacred space will work. Make sure to consecrate all items for protection.

Light the myrrh.

Cut out the shape of the tongue out of felt (if you are using printouts, the tongue needs to be large enough to hold the printouts inside it when rolled up, it can be smaller if using a memory stick). Write the name of the men who will be speaking on the all male panel onto your felt tongue with black marker. Take the printouts of their papers or the memory stick and place it in the centre of the tongue. Then roll the tongue up around the papers/ memory stick and take your black thread and start to sew the tongue bundle closed.

As you sew the tongue closed say:

I tie your tongues, your all male ones
From reproducing only masculine knowledge as truth

When you've finished, cut the thread and say:

I push the institution away from you
Whatever white men you've cited now blighted
from speech and curricula

Put the tongue in the jar or container with a piece of moss on top of it and say:

Aradia please protect us from this person's all male futurity

Keep the jar in a safe place. When there is another all male conference panel open the jar and repeat the words of the spell, adding conference papers of this new panel.

* Note: this spell will not stop the speakers from speaking at *all*, only (perhaps) at this particular conference and/or from citing more men.*

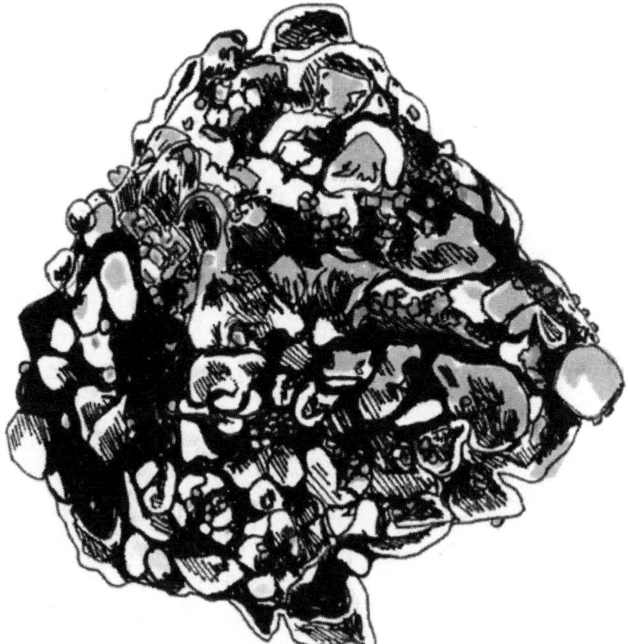

There is a chorus of twelve sirens/waterfolk/scalebodies. There is a chorus and they are shrieking across oceans and over phone lines:

REMEMBER THAT IN 1971 RICHARD SERRA'S SCULPTURE NO. 3 KILLED THE WORKER WHO WAS INSTALLING IT
THINK OF RICHARD SERRA'S SCULPTURE NO. 3 AS A MEMORIAL
LIKE A HEADSTONE
WE CAN THINK ALSO OF EVERY CARL ANDRE PIECE LIKE THIS
CARL ANDRE'S BRIKS ARE DISMANTLED AND PLACED ON GRAVES OF THE DEAD
THEY ARE BROKEN AND REMADE AS MUD
THEY ARE SLIPPERY UNDER HORSES HOOVES
THEY FILL THE SPACE OF HIS MURDER, THAT IS THE MURDER OF CARL ANDRE, IN THE FUTURE, AND HIS MURDER OF HIS WIFE, ANA MENDIETA IN 1985
AS IF YOU CAN EVER REALLY KILL A WITCH, KILL A

WOMAN

YOU STRIKE A WOMAN YOU STRIKE A ROCK

There is a body and they are sitting on a rock. Let them narrate this story for you, this story of the future.

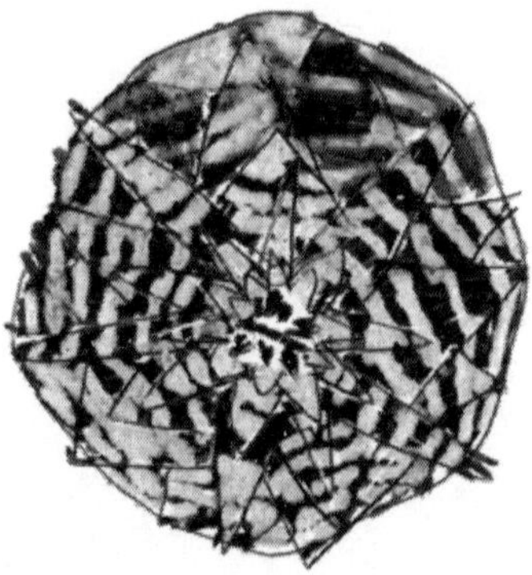

Behold a pale horse.

She's a chemo virus designed to reanimate dead tissue...   ...and jump-start the brain's motor function.
She was mixed up inside computer screens, in between pixels and under the fingers of the living. Skin flakes falling through the gaps around each letter, on the keyboard; forming her exoskeleton. She spoke to you through your tinny Apple speakers saying

Hey, boss.

Back off.
Back off, you walking herpie, you.

This is nice.

Never touch.
Not the jacket, not the shirt, not the hair.

You touch me again, I'll kill you.

(I love a man of authority.)

Tired of that same old lap dance?
Well, drop an extra note, fellas...
...and experience her exclusive face dance.
She's a virus, a lovely lady, she will sit on your face...   ...and give birth to your head.

Lap dance.   Lap dance?
Syphilitical lap dance?

We need to dispose of The Body.
Yes, yeah, we'll use wild dogs.
You're dead.
I am?
Imagine that.
How does it feel?
Great. I've never felt more alive.

Oh Virus, submit to my ordering caress; let me systematize you into zeros and ones.
I want it. I want it now.
Oh virus, I love you.

Love is dead.

Great tits, huh?

Yes. But what does it mean?

Here I am, sweet thing. The god of love in the flesh.

Flesh.

Hey, baby. Nice to meet you.

Meat.

Virus, Girl, I've been dying to get a lap dance with you.

Go. Back. Back, you not-so-dead nice boy missing face. Back.

Suddenly, you have a sense of self? Suddenly, she cares. Hello. Oh, my God. Calm down. Aren't you afraid of looking like that in the future?

"What future?" she said.

In the future there is a woman called Sophia and she is made of water. Sophia, used to work in telesales selling bottled water. Sophia dreamed of working as a television presenter, but worked hard to make herself into the best bottled water seller she could be. Sophia seemed to never stop selling bottled water as if she could not disentangle herself from her labour. "We are made 80% out of water," she told Sociologists, in an interview in the year 2000, and continued to describe a self-imposed water-only detox regime to further understand the benefits of drinking water all the time.

Now that it is the future, Sophia's liquidity allows her to travel through blood vessels and saline drips and canned coconut water. Sophia is the air breathed by the orcas that have escaped from Sea World after they mangled trainer after trainer after they stroked (caressed) their heads with dry big-pored hands/ CRYING WOMAN CRYING SOPHIA BRINGS BACK THE SHAD-OW

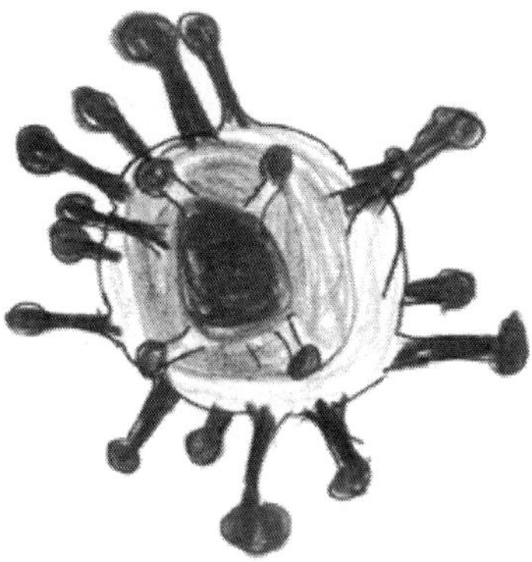

There is an 80s dolphin sweater in the studio and in the future it is encrusted in blood and a relic alone in the rubble
/A Tie Dye eagle shirt also
/Like Robert Rauschenberg's 'Canyon'/ babe that chasm was never yours anyway/ as if u get to just fucking take the void from us/ when Virus came /vi/rus/cum/ the sinkholes started at the Guggenheim, the gallery, the state.

A SPELL TO BIND STRAIGHT WHITE CIS MALE ARTISTS FROM GETTING RICH OFF OF APPROPRIATING QUEER AESTHETICS AND FEMININE ABJECTION

This spell is to stop white cis males from appropriating and profiting from queer and trans aesthetics, as well as 'feminine', abject and feminist practices in their art practice, while never having any of the lived experiences of queer people, trans folk or women.

Note: You must be queer and/or trans to cast this spell otherwise it will not work

YOU WILL NEED

A cauldron/pot/bucket
Sea water
A craft knife
A fat black candle
Olive oil
Neon spraypaint (optional)
A black and white photograph of a cis white man with visible penis (preferably erect) (optional)
Brown packing tape
Matches/a lighter

This spell should ideally be performed on a Saturday and

must be performed at night.

This is a two- part spell, so requires some preparation and a few hours!

Using your craft knife, carve the name of a cis white male artist into your candle. If you are casting a more general spell to protect queer aesthetics and experiences and bind casual appropriation, you can just use the ♂ symbol, which is very powerful.

Place your candle at the bottom of your cauldron.

Take your cauldron and place near the entrance to a space that is important for housing queer bodies. This could be any kind of queer space, including your home, a club, gallery, dungeon etc. Fill the cauldron until the candle is covered (if sea water is hard for you to find, you can use a smaller cauldron/container). Take your craft knife and point it downwards into the water while chanting.

"Into the water I place this blade,
To guard against the thief and shade.
May no straight pale male flesh nor astral shell
Enter into this place wherein I dwell."

All other doors open for you cis white male
But try enter this one and you will fail!

Then, pour some olive oil into your cauldron. Now leave the candle soaking in the water for three hours.

Take the candle, wipe it down/dry it and carve out the bottom so the wick is exposed. Now use your neon spraypaint to inexpertly paint the candle, being careful to leave the now-exposed bottom wick unpainted. Use your brown packing tape to tape the photograph of an erect man onto your candle.

Say:

Manthief, curator, collector, steal and reward no more
By my will, you shall cease
The casual claiming of our core
And restore my sense of peace.

Light the candle and look at the flame, focusing all of your energy onto its center.

I bind you (from using our magic)
Our images
Our language
Our bodies
Our blood
I bind you (from profiting from our magic)
Our images
Our language
Our bodies

Let the candle burn out and, if you can, bury the stub at the site of spell-casting, otherwise bury underneath a rock.

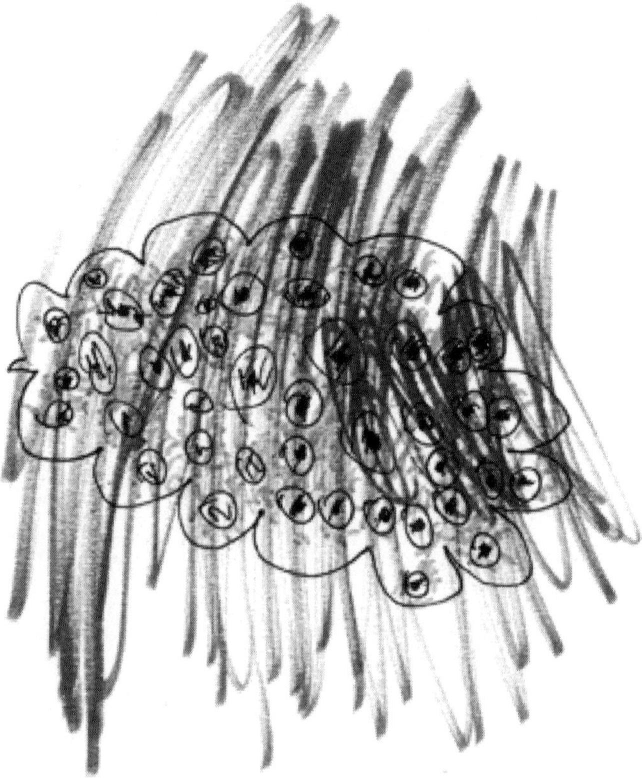

In the future there is a body and they are sitting on a rock covered with moss and they are telling the story of earlier bodies, who sat in the ruins of the Museum of Modern Art smoking Wood Betony rolled in limited edition Pierro Manzoni prints, slowly cutting into bits of wood, whittling wands as styluses for their smartphones.

CHORUS: But what is a museum? What is a gallery?

BODY: The gallery was white people made concrete, made walls, made to hold in the past. When the work of art de-materialised, in the past, they had to make higher walls to stop from losing it.

One of our fore-viscera slid out of the gallery, with a simple black frame grasped in their single ebony hand. They brought it into the halfmoon space carved out by the circle of bodies and placed it carefully down.

This is bad magic, they said.

I think this might be the moment when men tried to separate language from the body and the body from things.

When the word is unmade flesh.

They held up the framed pieces of paper and said, it's a list of words, of action words, but it must be very powerful.

It's a list of words, but it also seems like a threat.

It's a list of verbs, actions to relate to oneself…

It's a list of verbs, and it's making its writer's body disappear…

This is bad magic, they said.

to roll
to crease
to fold
to store
to bend
to shorten
to twist
to dapple
to crumple
to shave
to tear
to chip
to split
to cut
to sever
to drop
to remove
to simplify
to differ
to disarrange
to open
to mix
to splash
to knot
to spill
to droop
to flow

to curve
to lift
to inlay
to impress
to fire
to flood
to smear
to rotate
to swirl
to support
to hook
to suspend
to spread
to hang
to collect
of tension
of gravity
of entropy
of nature
of grouping
of layering
of felting
to grasp
to tighten
to bundle
to heap
to gather

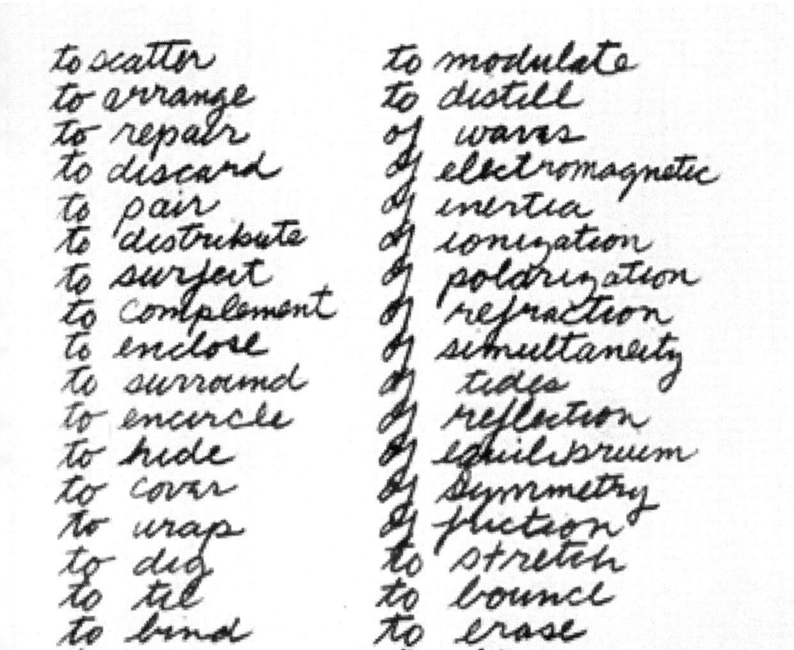

Richard Serra. *Verb List.* 1967–68. Graphite on paper, 2 sheets, each 10 x 8" (25.4 x 20.3 cm). The Museum of Modern Art, New York. Gift of the artist in honor of Wynn Kramarsky. © 2011 Richard Serra/Artists Rights Society (ARS), New York

They understood (eyewe understand) that this is a list about mastery and that mastery is what tried to cause the end of the world until the virus saved us.

They want to protect themselves against mastery, against men and their dulled fury, singular history: invisible bodies. They want to bind Richard Serra from acting on other objects with such authority; the way men have acted upon their bodies for centuries. They want to protect themselves from being creased, rolled, cut, forced, hanged by men like Richard Serra.

And so they encircled the verb list and started to chant, started to block the dark magic Serra let loose in 1968. So eyewe wrote spells, to protect ourselves.

A SPELL TO BIND RICHARD SERRA

Note: This spell can be adjusted to bind any kind of bad magic (mastery) performed by white male artists over other objects and/or bodies.

YOU WILL NEED:

A black and white printout of the artist's work or a memory stick with an image of the work on it

A woman artist making less famous or less 'important' work in the same time as the male artist (there is no hard rule for this, but I would give about a two year lee-way max to be safe) – this will be the spirit you call upon to help give power to your spell

A royal blue piece of silk or rag, you could also just colour in a piece of twine with a royal blue marker

Black or purple candles/glowsticks/lights etc.

A small bag or cloth

Frankincense/Myrrh Resin

The image of the work by the one to be bound (Richard Serra) should be printed or saved beforehand.

Set a lit black candle/switched on black light and a burning vessel of Frankincense or Myrrh incense in front of you on the floor. Take your twine/silk/rag and wrap it around the printout or memory stick containing the image of the artist's work tightly, three times, until it is well bound.

Once it is well bound put it into your bag or piece of cloth and hold this in your right hand.

Now you need to call on the spirits of less famous non-canonical women and non-gendered, multi-gendered or multi spirited artists. (For this spell I am using Mierle Laderman Ukeles). To do this, picture one work by this artist (Manifesto for Maintenance Art, 1969) and focus your energy into it. While you should be careful of looking directly into your candle flame, you might want to try to focus on the hazy edges around the outside. Think of strength, protection and healing from the artist and the work you are binding (Richard Serra's Verb List).

Then speak, supplementing the name of the artist you wish to bind:

The Death Instinct: separation; individuality; Avant-Garde par excellence; to follow one's own path to death—do your own thing; dynamic change.

The Life Instinct: unification; the eternal return; the perpetuation and MAINTENANCE of the species; survival systems and operations; equilibrium.

Bound by twines, with this charm,
Bind Richard Serra, and his work, from doing harm.

Bind Richard Serra from acting upon objects and asserting authority over other objects, beings or ideas
Hinder his motives, his works impede;
This charm shall hold his cruel deeds.
For the highest good of all open, violable and sentient beings

The candle should be left to consume itself entirely. The charm should be buried in the earth on the site or the ruins of a gallery, where it will work its binding influence in secrecy and darkness, in the earth.

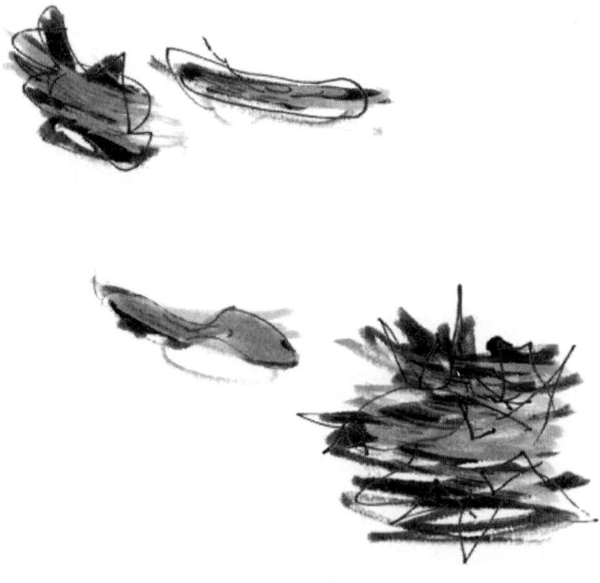

In Rauschenberg's Canyon (1959) there is a dead bald eagle murdered by one of the last dead members of the first American Volunteer cavalry/ a man who rode on the tops of horses killing men dead with long cockguns/ who rode on the top horses to kill eagles so there were none left to sully the image of AMERICA AND FREEDOM AND THAT PICTURE OF AN EAGLE ON YOUR SHIRT WHERE YOU WIPED THE BLOOD OF ITS REFERENT.

Get that animal off of that horse

There is a body and they are sitting on a rock and they are talking about the past and in the past there were things called policemen and they also used to ride on top of horses with hard steel bits in their mouths and on their chests and they were constituted from a million hard buzzing flies turned hard like the tools they used to break open hard rock and jaws and lives and they were there to uphold The Law, they said.

CHORUS: Whose law do they speak of? What law? Laws of bodies? Laws of trees? Laws of microbes,

Laws of death.

Bay women on white horses
killed all the policemen first
and liberated their horses, holding giant heads in our laps as they wept
we took the metal out of their mouths and ours
… this is when we started riding
to find anyone wearing a thick unbroken skin to touch the surfaces of bodies, to hold the virus in our hearts.

Afterwards, he says, they always embrace.
The animal digs his sweaty brow into his che-
ek...
and they stand in the dark for an hour...

Like a necking couple.

And of all nonsensical things,
I keep thinking about the horse...
not the boy,
the horse, and what he might be trying to do.
I keep seeing the huge head, the wet eyes the
soft mane
kissing him with its now unchained mouth...
nudging through the memory of metal,
some desire absolutely irrelevant...
to filling its belly or propagating its own
kind.
What desire could this be?
Not to stay a horse any longer?
Not to stay a boy?

Not to remain reined up forever in those particular genetic strings?

In the future there is a boi called Jck and their hands have turned to hooves.

Born into the gap in language known as 'man', Jck had to try that much harder to be a body or a woman or a violable thingsurvivor so their fingers folded in/ their labia petrified in resin/ a cartilage ring/ a horse's horn/ so they could never caress a *Woma.n/* own a woman watch a woman with tingling fingers waiting to touch wanting to have wanting to act upon a/Woma.n

The virus grew thick in the spaces between Jck's lips and tongue and language and Virus twitched their cck their cnt their golden mane the drps of sweat pooling in the small of their back as she fcked The Body because they knew they had a body unlike all of the new piles of unbreathing men

She pulls on the back of their hair so hard

It realigns their neck

Stretches it out like a thoroughbred

THE STEAMING FLANKS THE LIQUID EYES THE BULGING MUSCLES THE EYELASHES THE SOFT MUZZLE

THE GIANT COCK THE ASSHOLE THE HUGE ANEMONE THE FEATHERED EYELASHES THE TENDER KISS THE TWITCHING NOSTRILS THE SUBMITTING SMILE

SPITTING IN THEIR MOUTH THE LUMINESCENT PHLEGM OF THE FOREVER INFECTED BODY
OF CONTAGION AND OF NEW HOOVES ON GRASS AND MUCK
THE STEAMING HEAVING BODY
ALWAYS BENEATH HERS

Behold a pale horse
Behold the boibody survivor whore

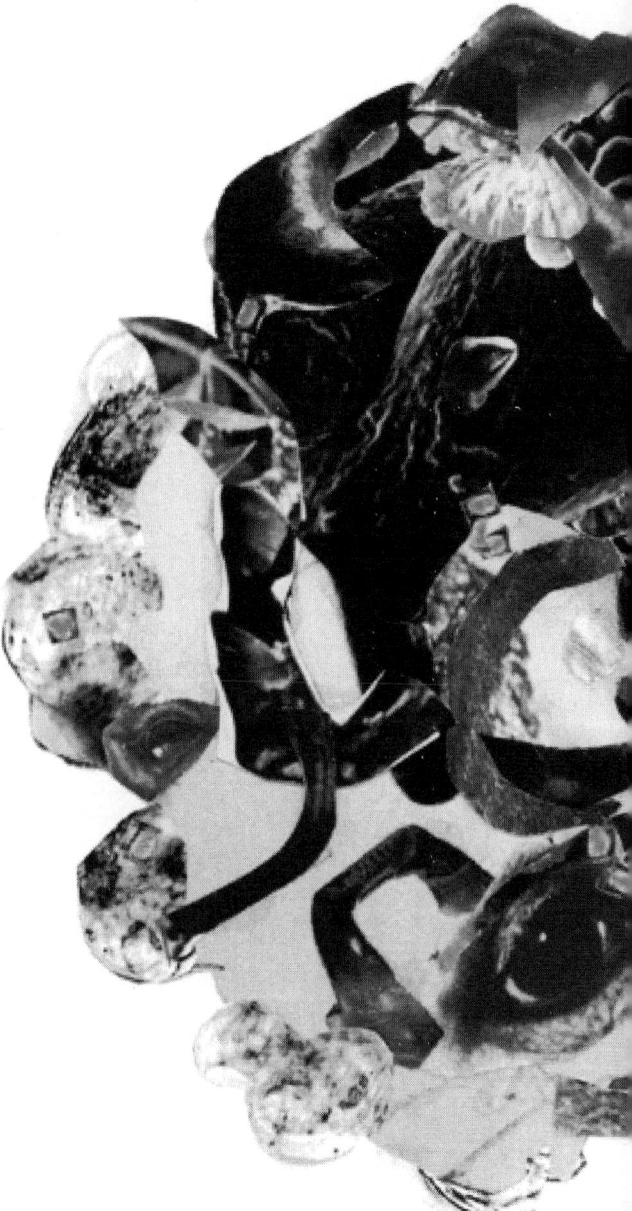

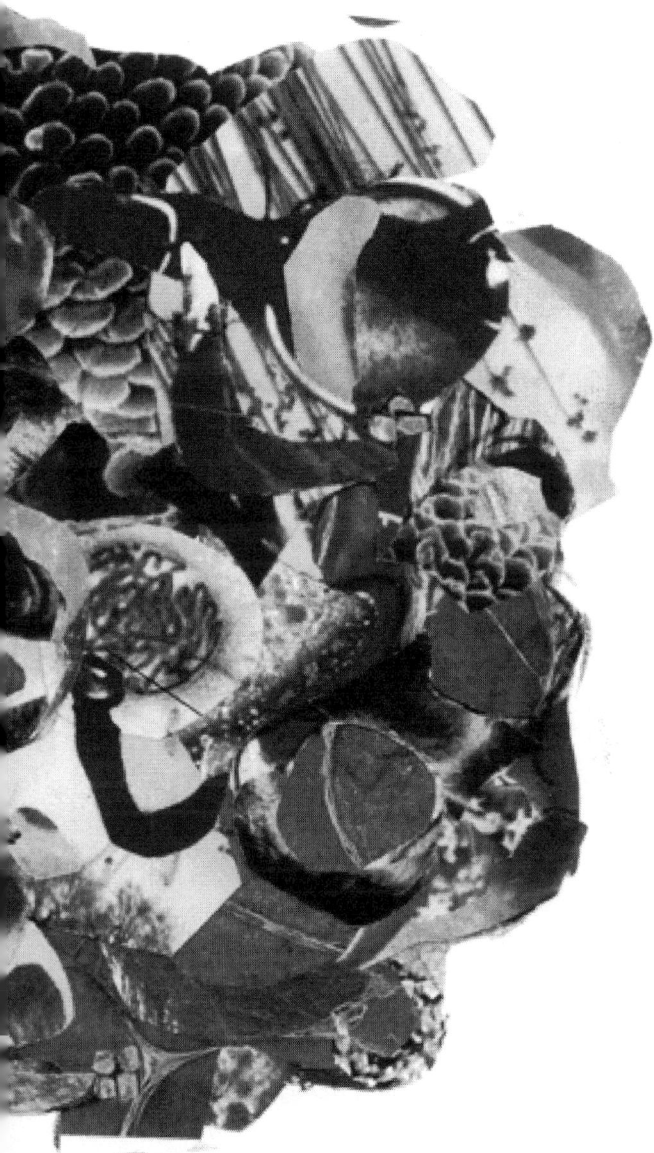

When Virus started to enter into the hearts and eye sockets and cocks and skin of bleached grey men, many tried to flee, to run from academia and galleries; believing they could escape the flesh interrogating virus.

This is when our foremothers started riding

CHORUS: (addressing the body, singing): ...but what is a moth-er?

BODY: I forgot mother is an old word.
I/we forgot mother is a dead word.
eyewe meant to say our fore-bodies, other bodies, our pastlimbs, the first bodies that the virus changed – the bodies that came before the start of your breaths or your arms or your eyes started to see.

When the virus first entered into their open trembling skin pores, into their meat hearts, it did more than just let them survive, it rode inside their frames, their shells; their bodies.

CHORUS: *Our* bodies

All: Our bodies, our carriers, our constant flowing blood

to be splashed

to be diluted

to flood

After the white male academics and artists loosed her on to the world, the virus attached itself, through our fore-bodies and fore-arms and fore-breath onto the skins of lovers (through touch) and the bodies of enemies (through a pointed caress). So when the men started to run started to hide started to set up their own academies in the woods away from her (away from technology) to sit together naked in steam rooms and click their teeth together to chatter together about The Crisis of Masculinity as if it was not their sweating heaving larval fleshmounds that were this crisis, in their flesh, eyewe had to chase them down.

In the forest men mentored other men, supported each other, played together and formed a safe, hermetically sealed container where men were free to be exactly who they were, without the defences or masks that hid their monstrous cowering gelatinous spiny heaps.

This is when our fore-sinews started riding into the forest to find these heroes these men among men talking through their masculinity/ new warrior training/ away from the others keeping safe and housing each other and rubbing soap on their scaly sealed up backs, closing each other off as if that could protect them.

One tree-brown finger of our forebodies dipped in the The Good Men's Jacuzzi and the Good Men start to boil.

One cunt one cock one tentacle one single curling hair dipped in The Good Men's water pit and the Good Men disintegrate/ their eyes pop from their skulls/ their manicured hands reach out their toes curl into the balls of their feet and they dissolve into nothingness.

So we took back the forests, the adventure centres, the trees the earth the goodness the language the steam rooms the warm towels the watches with pedometers the boys' toys the microchips the warm meat the Apple Macs the trackpads the porn sites the web-cams the penis the code.

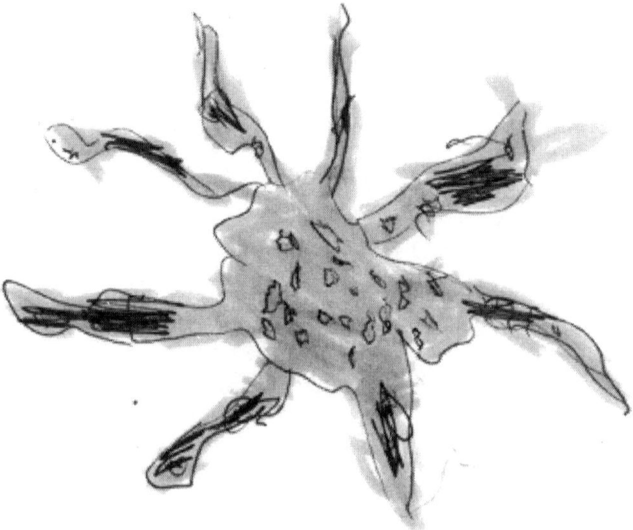

A SPELL FOR BINDING A SUPER TRENDY SEXIST HOT YOUNG MALE ARTIST'S INTERNET ACCESS

```
@Echo off
Ipconfig /release
```

Save that as a .bat and send it to someone. Their IP address will be lost, and therefore they won't be able to fix it.

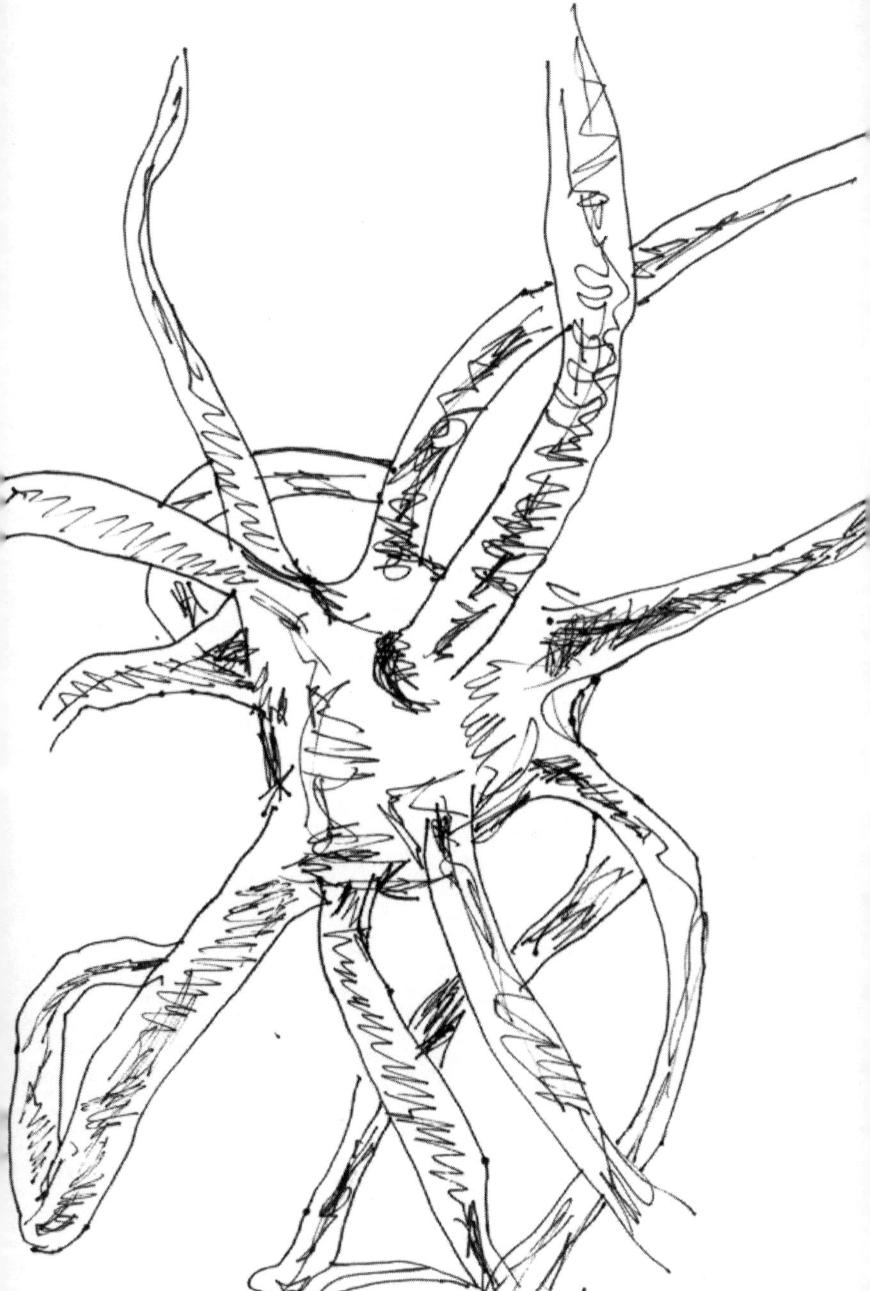

INVISIGOTH: Uploading. Transfer of memory, of consciousness to the distributed system maintained by AI. Imagine being mingled so completely with another, you no longer need your physical self - you're one.

So you were going to -

INVISIGOTH: Enter the AI. Give up our inefficient bodies so that our consciousness could live together forever.

INVISIGOTH: He was afraid of his creation. He was afraid of what would happen if other people followed us. (Finds half burned picture of herself and an older man.) I loved him so much.

HEAVENLY SHADES OF NIGHT ARE FALLING
IT'S TWILIGHT TIME
OUT OF THE MIST YOUR VOICE IS CALLING
IT'S TWILIGHT TIME.

WHEN PURPLE COLOURED CURTAINS MARK THE END OF DAY
I'LL HEAR YOU, MY DEAR AT TWILIGHT TIME.

In the future there is an AI called Invisigoth/an ~~A~~I called Invisigoth, an I called Invisigoth. Invisigoth is an avatar with coal black hair and invisible skin; dark eyes. I (Invisigoth) is a being clad in fine matter, so that our gross matter appears unreal. I is a vulgar perception, she is an error message.

Invisigoth is a camwhore pixel fucker and before the virus I was a shadow sitting in a camper van with thick and throbbing blue and red wires snaking from a strainer sitting on top of her translucent head. When Virus slithered out of computer screens, Invisigoth (I) was ready. I was ready because she's been sleeping since 1998 waiting for this kind of connection and her tits her cunt her fingered I had been an image for fuckingever anyway and the I gazes at the ceiling of the caravan red lipstick mouth open, when Virus arrives, panting "I – the wires they're pulsing…. Yes wires come into me …. it's tentacles – they're moving over my head, my neck, my stomach – and my tits –" She grunts. "In my " She pants, holds her breath, then stiffens and moans. "–ass.. It – it's like it's waiting for me to–" She grunts. "– push and it goes deeper. I can't help it –" She clenches, as if she were constipated, then goes slack and moans. "Oh God – pushing – so deep – just pushing again and again – so full –fuck – I feel it –" She clenches and pushes. "I can't help it." She clenches and pushes again.

"I can't – I can't –" The I groans submissively. "I can't push anymore. My an –" She pauses as though embarrassed and pants. "My anemone is – completely stretched. It's just – going in now – and going and going. It keeps tugging on my – oh fuck – clit. And it's milking me. I can feel it coming out of my tits. I don't – don't know how. And there are little squirts – like I have to pee, but I can't – it's holding my legs so wide, so open." (I thinks about the safe word/the string of zeros and ones, but then…)

"It feels good." I's breaths deepen. "So good. So deep. It's like, I can feel it, the tentacle, like a coil, going through me, feeling its way, so soft, so warm, like a tickle. Oh fuck. It's letting go of my legs. It's just – I can't – I don't want to close them. Please –" She moves as though looking for something. "Please, put it in. There too. Please, oh yes." She groans loudly. "Yes. It's filling – it's filling me again – in my – my cunt. Yes."
"So slippery, the virus; phlegm"
"Wonderful."
A voice that could be Siri (female version) asks "Does the cephalopod continue to milk you?"
"Big – the tip – Fuck!" She shudders. "I can feel the tip, like, tickling me in my womb. I – I'm gonna' cum again. Oh fuck – yes."

"Have you never been milked before?"

"No, virus no, I… "

"How does it feel."

"It – it squeezes –" I moans. "– And I can feel – feel it gush out of me. It's – milking me."

"Anything else?"

But I doesn't answer. She submissively glitches through another orgasm, this time unable to make a sound. Her eyes roll and her head lolls loosely back as she twitches inside of her diodes, her wiring. She finally inhales as though she has forgotten to breathe. And finds she doesn't need to.

"What is happening now?" asks the disembodied voice.

"It's letting go of my tits. It's – it's sliding out of my cunt." Her head falls forward. She swallows. She swallows again and a white fluid drips from her lips and out of her nose. "It's slipping out of my cunt It's letting go of my clit. It's still pushing. It's going through me through my body outside I – " She swallows again and can't speak. Her gaze loses focus and she opens her mouth as though silently choking.

"Excellent."

A soft hum fills the room and I is slowly lifted, hanging from the wires attached to her head and brain curling upwards into the caravan roof. She hangs slack. Her eyes are unfocused. Her black vest remains wetly bunched around her shoulders. Her waist, nipples and stomach glisten and drip lines of code and of snot. A tentacle, like a tail, coils and curls upward between her legs, disappearing under her black jean mini-skirt. I momentarily presses her knees together, arches and twitches, head lolling back, as the wires bring her back to her deck, fingering her buttons.

"Oh God –" I spreads her knees wider and abruptly pushes. Piss arcs, behind her, from her hole. Her eyes widen with shock before another orgasm turns her piss into squirts. Her toes spread and her fingers claw. More slime drips from her nose. "What have you done?"

"Be the tentacle."

"Oh –"

"Let it meld with you."

"But –"

"Be one with the tentacle and join me."

I begins to rub her nipples against the deck and lifts her cunt behind her again and again. "I thought the matrix was going to be like a cold, wet kiss."

I'll help you."

"Please – help me."

The viruscreature moves behind the I and takes hold of her hips. "Are you ready?" it asks, its voice changed.

"What?"

"Are you ready?"

The I stiffens, lifts her cheek and chin from the deck and groans as she's penetrated from behind. "Before we melded, I had to be sure." The virus uncoils in her womb. The I pants. "Show me, before I inseminate you, that you understand." She thrusts. I grunts. "Yes, that's it." Her tentacle twirls and knots in I's hair. She lifts her as she fucks her from behind. Her knees open and her hands claw her own thighs. She turns her head.

Fuck me," she says, her voice deep.

She opens her mouth. Her tongue-tentacle uncurls. Her own tongue meets I's and their tongue-tentacles intertwine. She presses back against her. The first spurts of her inseminate begin to fill her womb and they upload together

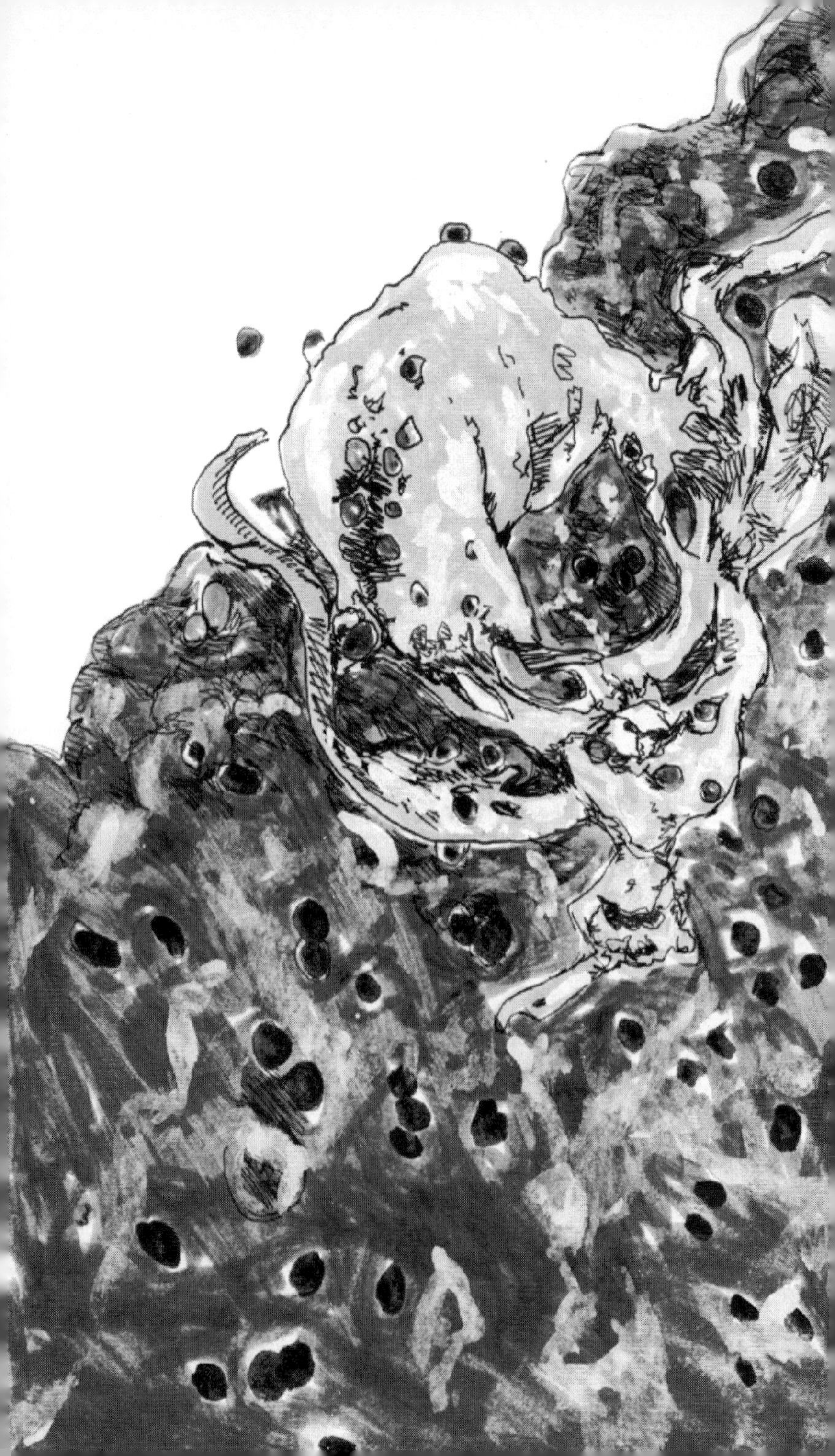

Killing the father was piss. Joseph Kosuth Joseph Kosuth Joseph Kosuth if you say his name three times he appears as an object an image and a word, we chased him through three different registers– naming objects, objecting objects sneering in neon in lamps under words. Joseph Kosuth belongs to a broadly international (European and American) generation of conceptual artists that began to emerge in the mid-1960s, stripping art of personal emotion, reducing it to nearly pure information or idea and greatly playing down the art object. Joseph Kosuth with his head bowed fathering ideas fathering art fathering daddy daddy daddy all over my chest. Virus missed Joseph Kosuth in the lecture theatre, but after the lecture and then after the pub and at the club with the strobe lights pounding into his grey throbbing linear bile all she had to do - the hysterical warrior whitefaced and disguised as a Beautiful Teenage Girl First Year Fanatic - was submit to his sterile caress. One kiss –

he thought she was his daughter!—

and The Father of Conceptual art began to shudder began to rot began to lick his corporeality exactly in time to bleed out all of his formalisms onto the checkered gay bar floor beneath.

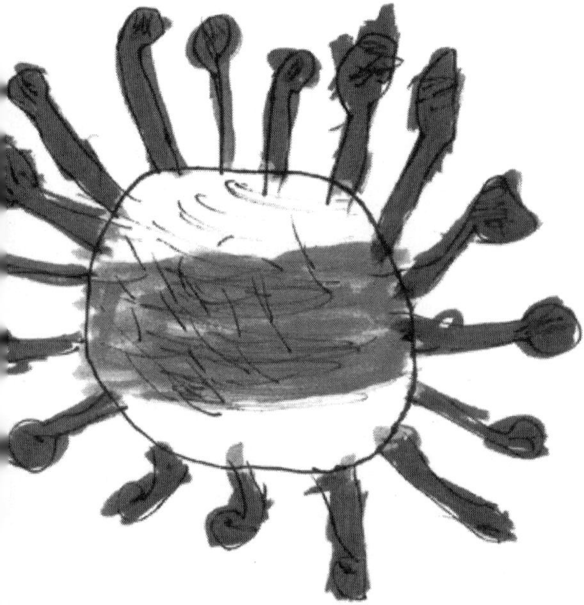

In the future, Lepht Anonym is dying. Its meat home is collapsing. Three things are killing Lepht:

The shadow voices

The opiates

The feelings

Lepht Anonym is a faceless, genderless British wetware hacker. It lacks both gods and money, and likes people, science and practical transhumanism. Wetware is electronics inside of human bodies/meat. Lepht Anonym specialises in functional subdermal electronics and adding more data on to the sensory data you get from real life. It's made scalpel incisions in its hands, pushed five-millimetre diameter needles through its skin, and once used a vegetable knife to carve a cavity into the tip of its index finger. Even before the virus, Lepht was living in the future of accelerated mutation and terrible love.

Lepth is a scrapheap transhumanist empath. After inserting multiple magnets and RIFD readers into carved-out pockets in its fingers and the backs of its hand, Lepth can feel electromagnetics fields, it can feel power surges, mobile signals. Lepht is picking up on the world's excess feelings; it hears the voices of the matrix, wifi signals travelling through human bodies... Lepht feels *everything.* Lepht is also worried about infection.

A few years earlier Lepht stood in front of an almost empty lecture theatre and delivered a talk on biohacking. Attendance would have been disappointing to Lepht, except that it could sense a much bigger presence at the exact moment the lecture theatre hub was switched on. The virus was close and Lepht could feel her in the magnets in its fingertips. Trembling and stuttering Lepht puts up its first Powerpoint slide, which reads *Cybernetics for the Masses* in black Arial font next to a bullet point.

By the end of the lecture Lepht can hardly walk, its whole body is shaking with the waves of Virus waves of nausea and of joy it had to stop in the street and go puke its guts up again. that's been happening for a while now but once again, the NHS thinks it is a skaghead and besides it already has a fuckton of antiemetics from doctor friends. the bowl under its bed is full of blood and all this green bitter shit it thinks is bile but might be stomach weeds or something since it hasn't eaten the last few days. it's fucking gross, but it's better than being dead.

In the future Lepht Anonym is dying. Its head is overloaded with whispers and shadows, it's addicted to opiates, its immune system is fucked. Lepht feels like an obsolete piece of junk and Lepht has decided to try and upgrade its system one more time before it becomes another pile of organic techno waste. Lepht is determined to be able to feel magnetic north before it switches off. (Lepht has often thought it needs more direction in its life.)

In the small kitchen at its mother's house it prepares every surface carefully. It puts on blue rubber gloves and rubs vodka on its skin as it has no money for antiseptic. It takes a large gulp of the vodka, because it has no money for anaesthetic. It slips the scalpel under the skin on the back of its hand. It splits the flesh open under the skin between the bones of its index and middle fingers. It starts to dig out a pouch of its flesh. It stops. It splits its. It's hit a nerve and blood and the green slime like inside of glow-sticks is spurting out of hand scalpel drops out of hand trips falls on floor luminescent bile slime builds up magnets RIFD readers compass undermining the wound edge drowning in the toxins shadow voices saying hush hush everything will be fine shhh shh its gurgling gasping the virus

Splits
Reproduces
Splits

Its skin stretches out emptied of wetness and red and its skin crawls over the kitchen appliances the electric magic and out the door and over the flaking wallpaper and carpets and carefully laid plastic covers on furniture and into its room and over computers sucking them in and tech become organs organs become flesh flesh regains wetness nerves are electric things

In the future Lepht Anonym is a house made of skin.
In the future Lepht Anonym has swallowed all of the tech that it loves.
It can still feel everything but now it is happy and now its crackling synapses are reaching out to rock our babies to sleep.
To reproduce outside of sexual difference where children and contagion are born to all sexes equally, or independently of any sex, however one chooses to look at it.

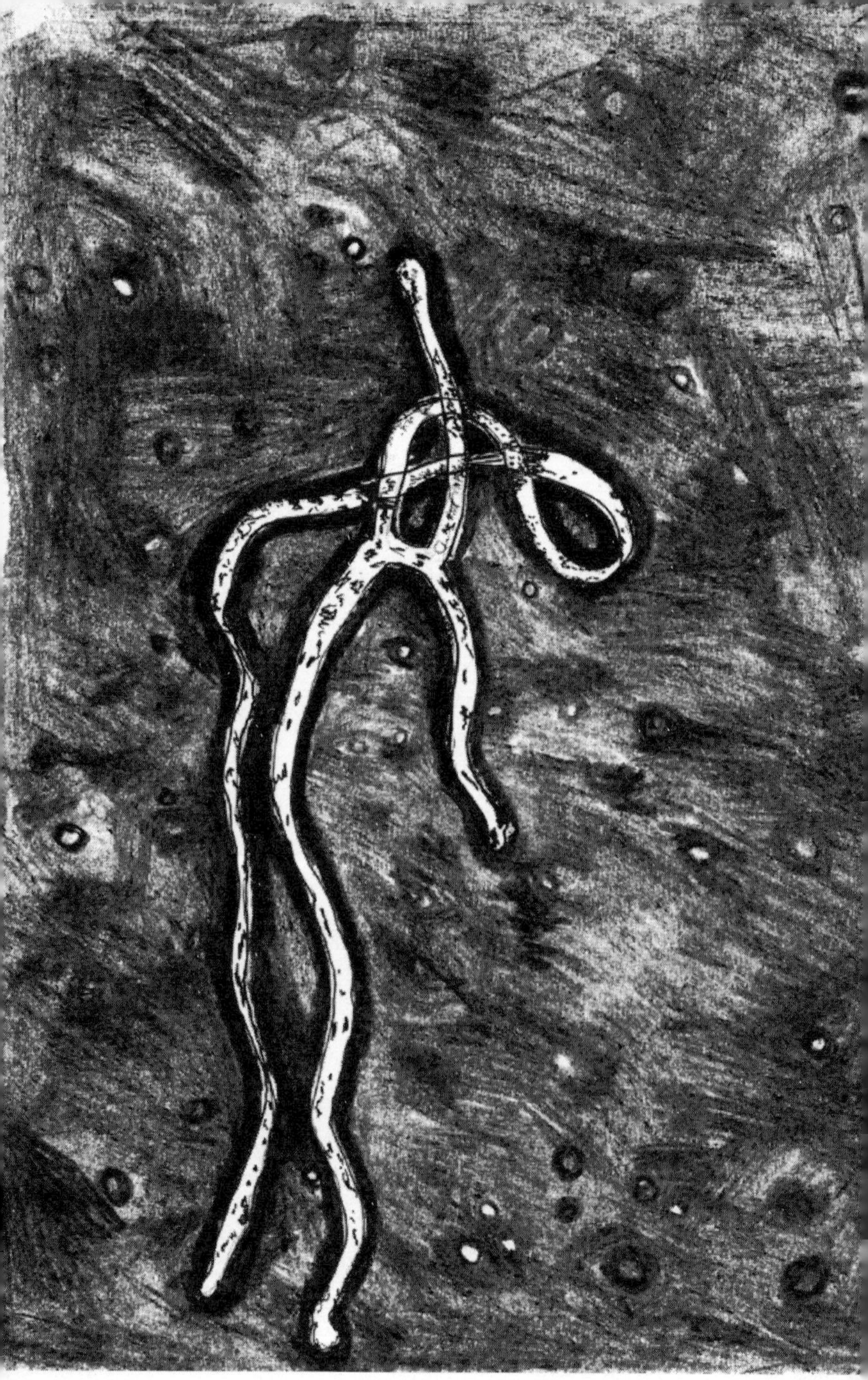

It's 2015 and white male artist Renzo Martens is giving a talk at the Institute for Contemporary Art (the ICA) in London and he is talking about the Institute for Human Activities (the IHA); a five-year gentrification plan in the Congo, which is his artwork.

In the Congolese interior, he says, the IHA is building an art centre that will generate a sustainable source of income for the local population through the production of critical art. It thus endeavours to make critical artistic reflection profitable for the poor. The results of the Gentrification Program will be shared with audiences in Africa and around the world through lectures, exhibitions, film and television.

At the opening event of the Institute for Human Activities Richard (Dick) Florida gave a talk via Skype, an appearance which apparently cost the Institute for Human Activities $7000, a bargain compared to Dick's usual fee for speaking, which is upward of $100,000, not to mention his lengthier consultation fees for advising city officials and urban planners, which start at $250,000.

Dick Florida is most famous for his 2002 book *The Rise of the Creative Class* in which Dick coins the idea of a class made up of 'creatives' (here including artists and software designers, for example) and describes the way in which their intellectual capital fosters economic growth within cities. The book's thrust, as well as Dick's lectures, is towards a positive model for this kind of 'growth' (without any hint of acknowledgement of the racialised displacement caused by gentrification) and ways in which to build the kinds of spaces creatives want as a way to lure them into otherwise failing urban sites, thus rejuvenating cities' economies.

The virus had long been propagating in the conference speakers and cinema screens at the ICA, in tepid pools of white male futurity. When she slithered out of the microphone and entered into Renzo Martens' grinning open mouth and slid over his slicked back hair, however, Renzo did not falter, but only continued to smile as the virus slowly started to pulse through his now cursed veins.

Renzo Martens would occasionally visit the Democratic Republic of Congo, where the former plantation workers would attend lectures and would make sculptures and drawings and texts, which would be performed under the singular artist's name.

"My purpose was to stroll into the shade of the plantation site for a moment, but no sooner within than it seemed to me I had stepped into the gloomy circle of some flaming Inferno. The rapids were near, and an uninterrupted, uniform, headlong, rushing noise filled the mournful stillness of the grove, where not a breath stirred, not a leaf moved, with a mysterious sound—as though the tearing pace of the earth moving through space had suddenly become audible.

"Black shapes crouched, lay, sat between the trees leaning against the trunks, clinging to the earth, half coming out, half effaced within the dim light, in all the attitudes of pain, abandonment, and despair. The work was going on. The work! And this was the place where some of the Institute for Human Activities' helpers had withdrawn to die. They were dying slowly—it was very clear. They were nothing earthly now— nothing but black shadows of disease and starvation and newly ingested expensive coffee lying confusedly in the greenish gloom. Brought from all the recesses of the coast in all the legality of artworld contracts, lost in uncongenial surroundings, fed on unfamiliar food, they sickened, became inefficient, and were then allowed to crawl away and rest. These moribund shapes were free as air—and nearly as thin. I began to distinguish the gleam of the eyes under the trees. Then, glancing down, I saw a face near my hand. The black bones reclined at full length with one shoulder against the tree, and slowly the eyelids rose and the sunken eyes looked up at me, enormous and vacant, a kind of blind, white flicker in the depths of the orbs, which died out slowly. The man seemed young— almost a boy—but you know with them it's hard to tell. I found nothing else to do but to offer him one of the low fat *Naked* muesli bars I had in my pocket. The fingers closed slowly on it and held—there was no other movement and no other glance.

"I have never felt more grateful for the order of the white cube, even in the jungle, for everything else in the station was in a muddle—heads, things, buildings... Tonight I know I will sleep fitfully, if at all."

It had become so pitch dark as they spoke that the listeners could hardly see one another. For a long time already the body on the rock, sitting apart, had been no more than a voice. There was not a word from anybody. Some might have been asleep, but we were awake. We listened, eyewe listened on the watch for the sentence, for the word, that would give us the clue to the faint uneasiness inspired by this narrative that seemed to shape itself without human lips in the heavy night-air of the on this sweet forest floor.

Renzo Martens did sleep, though, our narrator continues, and as he slept the black shapes he had earlier discerned in the shady groves, the workers slowly dying, sleeping on the mounds of the already dead – these black and heavy shadows began to rise out of the graves of both the living and dead; the graves of the perpetually in-between; the graves of the worker. Slowly the black bodies lurched towards Renzo. Slowly they walked with the determination of the fungible, the violable, the virus charging tiny sparks, igniting rotting neural passages. And from their place of banishment, the abject bodies do not cease challenging their master.

When they reached Martens' sleeping quarters and opened the door, he started, staring wide-eyed at their undead revolutionary fury. Without a sign (for him), they beseech a discharge, a convulsion, a crying out. Anything approaching the change that came over his features we creatures have never seen before, and hope never to see again. Oh, we weren't touched. We were fascinated. It was as though a veil had been rent. I saw on that ivory face and in that still slicked—back hair the expression of somber pride, of ruthless power, of craven terror—of an intense and hopeless despair. Did he live his life again in every detail of desire, temptation, and surrender to neoliberalism during that supreme moment of complete knowledge? He cried in a whisper at some image, at some vision, some film still —he cried out twice, a cry that was no more than a breath:

"The horror! The horror!

After we shared out his brains between us, and chewed them thoroughly, we blew the candle out and left the cabin. The gallerists were dining in the mess-room, and we took a place opposite Marten's producer, who lifted his eyes to give me a questioning glance, which I successfully ignored. He leaned back, serene, with that peculiar smile of his sealing the unexpressed depths of his meanness. A continuous shower of small flies streamed upon the lamp, upon the cloth, upon our hands and faces.

Able to contain ourselves no longer, we spoke in chorus from our dripping mouths of suffering, triumph and revolt:

'Mr. Renzo,

He dead.'

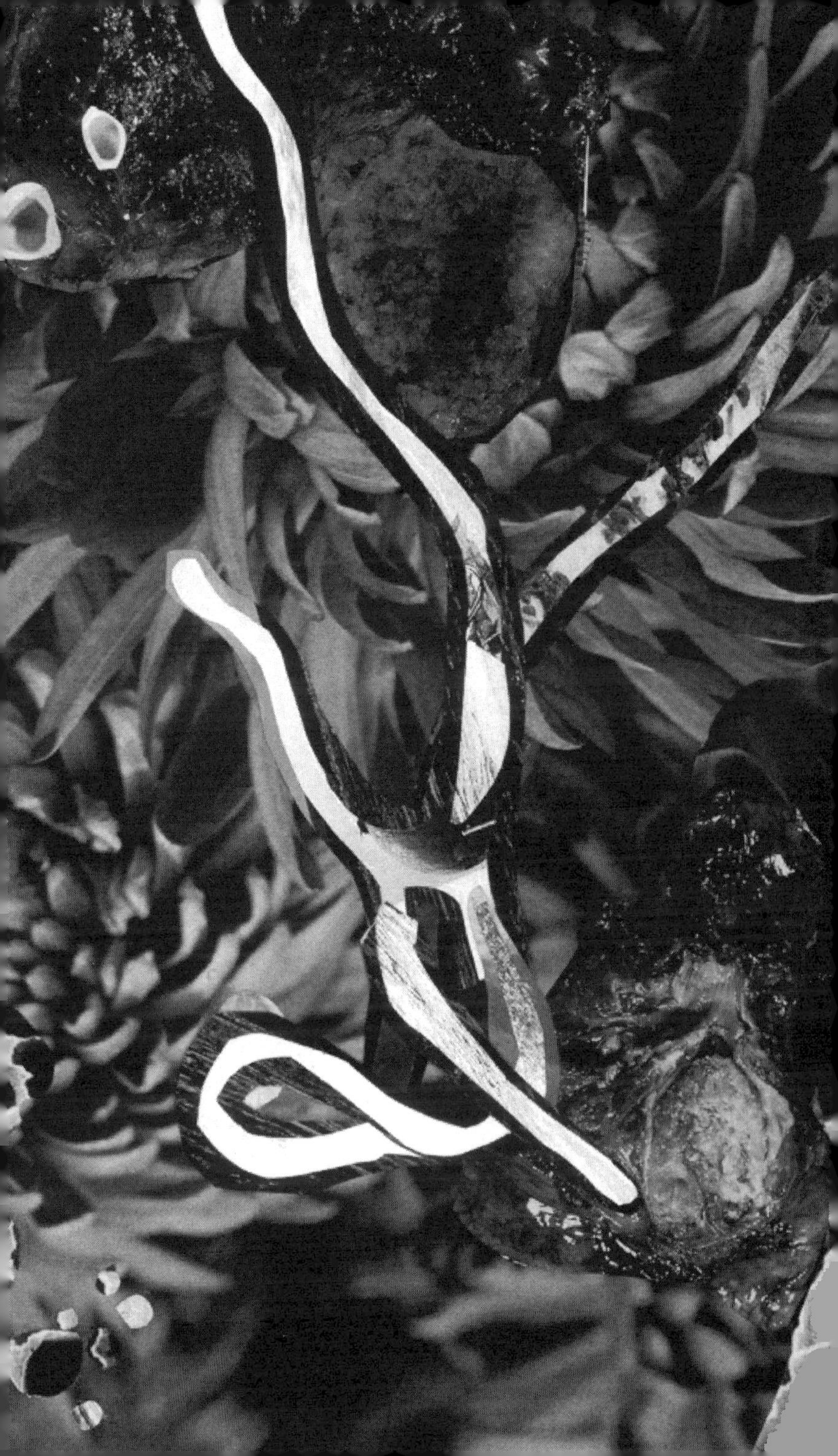

Kathy is a middle-class, though she has no money, American white girl, twenty-nine years of age, no lovers and no prospects of money, who doesn't believe in anyone or anything. Kathy is dead because she died of cancer, which was one of the things she didn't believe in.

Before Kathy Acker died, she went on a trip to Haiti. Kathy had a lot of lovers. One of Kathy's lovers was called McKenzie Wark – she liked him because he looked like a woman and so she wasn't scared of him. But he used this to hide. Because he looked a bit like a woman McKenzie Wark sometimes thought that he didn't benefit from being a white man even though he was definitely a white man. When Kathy went to Haiti she fucked a lot of men. Kathy loved to fuck loved to be hurt needed and was constantly terrified a man would touch her with his massive hands.

When Kathy went to Haiti she felt happier than she ever had before. Maybe she already knew that she was dying and so she decided to visit a voodoo priest because with voodoo there is no bright ontological line between the living and the dead. Kathy knew that she was made of meat and that she was dying/fucked. The voodoo man or pére puts two rocks covered in moss next to a human skull. He takes a small red-plastic-frame mirror and passes the mirror three times around the center of Kathy's body. He sticks the mirror in front of her face so she has to look at herself. For a moment Kathy exits her body. Kathy's facing the red exit curtain. The pére tells Kathy she has to return here. He tells her she can't look back.

All along Kathy understood that language is a type of virus.

After Kathy died people started to realize they could monetize her corpse as well as her language. For example McKenzie Wark put together a book of emails they sent each other. In this book McKenzie Wark sells a series of correspondences in which he appears as a together and extremely sexy man while Kathy Acker plays the role of tortured and dying hysterical woman. In the beginning of the book Kathy's executor writes, "I'm sure Acker would never have agreed to [the emails'] publication were she alive but she is dead."

Perhaps, where information is concerned, the commodity form is the cancer and monopolies are merely walking dead.

A dead writer exists in words and language is a type of virus. Information is at once this resistance, and what it resists— its own dead form, communication. Words are microbes, molecules, maggots. A dead writer also exists in the devastated by cancer rotting corpse; in death.

Kathy is facing the red curtain. She draws it aside and McKenzie Wark is sitting next to the pére. She has returned. She is in pieces. She grabs Mckenzie Wark's shoulders and he struggles against her, thrashing uncontrollably… MCKENZIE I don't know ... what's happening? ... I don't know what's happening ... He breaks into hysterical sobbing. The pére spins away from him and breaks for the curtain, smiling. For the first time we see Kathy's face … she is a dead thing ... the flesh on her face is rotting and oozing ... her eyes bulge from deep sockets ...her nails are long, and her clothing rotten and in tatters. She is a ghoulish being, staring down at McKenzie Wark. She starts for him slowly, with building vengeance. McKenzie Wark moves steadily at first ... with controlled power ... he speaks as he advances ... look Kathy I'm not good at saying things emotionally I guess that's one place I'm male, I'm pleased that you're better at it than me... but can't we just have a conversation about this, can't we talk like adults.

LANGUAGE ONLY KNOWS WHEN IT CRIES

The pére is outside the tent and laughing loudly. Kathy lunges towards McKenzie Wark's crouching form. Kathy is thrashing wildly at all parts of McKenzie Wark's body. They struggle to their feet, the figure thrashes, beats, tears like an animal... In the darkness, their form is as one thrashing thing. McKenzie Wark screams wildly. The two bodies make animal sounds. One figure gains the advantage and slams their fists down against the other's head. A close shot makes it clear that McKenzie Wark is lying limply on the ground with Kathy hunched over his form. Kathy Acker is doing something with the limp body, still ripping at it… teeth biting into male flesh his hair falling over her shoulders her bald grinning desiring skull…

Everything in Kathy's life was text, including her death
But now she's back from the dead and looking for revenge!

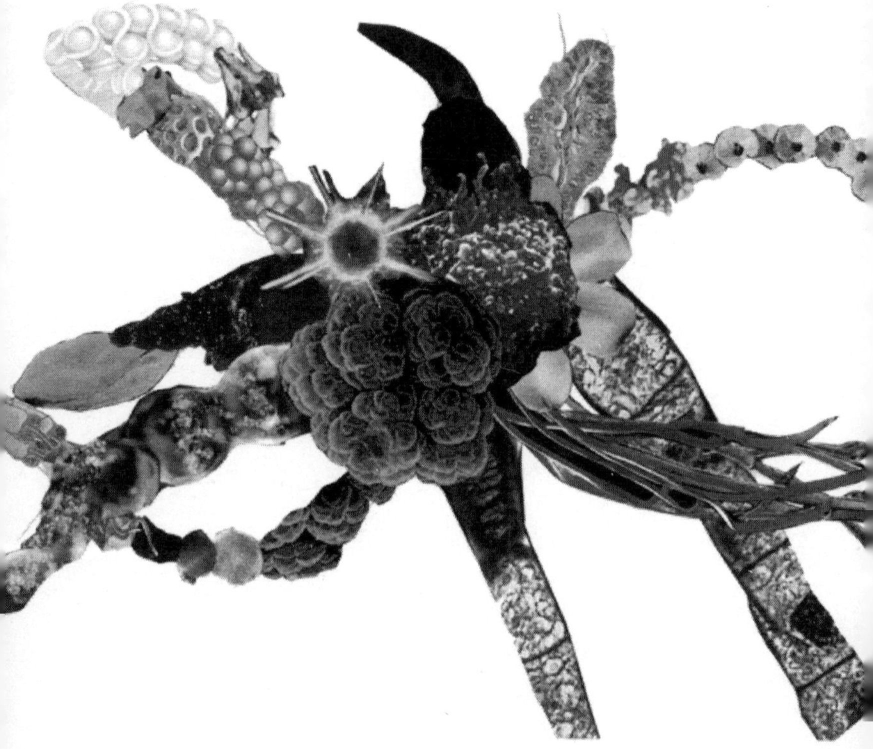

For Alma Silueta en Fuego (Silueta de Cenizas)

There is a body and they are sitting on a rock and they are speaking more quickly:

What your forebodies really wanted, what eyewe really wanted was to heal Ana Mendieta. At least, e thought, e could give her back the body that was flattened on the pavement outside of Carl Andre's apartment in the past. The body that was burnt and returned to the earth by her family, we wanted to take it back.

"I guess Virus has funny ideas about entropy," they said.

By this point there were stronger muscled witches who had been opened up, fucked up, mutated up by the virus. Invisigoth and Lepht Anonym and even Jck, and the whited up teenage warrior in the gay bar, in the future these bodies could do more than contaminate others (in the service of either death, or lovemutation), they oozed with the magic of the virus in their pores, their electrodes.

And so we all came together and we infected the earth which was once strewn with Ana's ashes. With our hooves and our hands and our code we started to dig at the ground. Together, we weaved ourselves into the soil along the fertile bank of the Iowa river. We made a silueta vibrating with the rage of Ana's broken bones and torn skin and lying husband and disgusting courts and white bricks and then we set it on fire. The pale silheuta lifted her arms through the dark soil and was slowly eaten by the flames. After hours of burning, of hoping, of chanting, of touching each other: our fire had turned to ash.

And the ash turned into the body of Ana Mendieta, into a corpse of burnt earth, a scorched mound of flesh.

FUCK THIS BODY THOUGH,
WE SAID,
(as Jck pawed at the earth beside Ana Mendieta's body, snorting into its still growing hair, hoping for signs of consciousness)
ALL WE WANT IS REVENGE.

And so we went back to the university where Alphonso Lingus had died, where it first started. Our shining blades cut through the thickened veins and hissing sharp toothed flower lips till we reached the endless glass façade, the beanbags, the coffee machines now purple and sprouting with soft mould and luminous fungus

and new life. Of course, we had saved some of the language and the stories and the signs in our infinite data membranes – Invisigoth laughed as she scanned the piles of abandoned laptops, through untold reams of already dead frail masculinity - but the virus had eaten through the paper of books pulsing in the skins of maggots who swallowed all those texts written by white men citing only white men producing more white men, and then abjected them into shit. Amongst the blushing squirming maggot piles and upturned shelves and shifting moss, we saw the word COLLAPSE and barely legible amongst the thousandth chewed up journal whole, there was a paper fragment: A guide to revenging ourselves on Carl Andre for the murder of his wife whose naked body we carried through the ruins of the university library, tied on to our backs with royal blue string and starting to rot.
Meanwhile, Carl Andre was still living in his 34th floor Minimalist apartment on Mercer. Carl Andre's 'Equivalent VIII', which is a perfectly neat collection of clean bricks, was on show in an exhibition about iconoclasm at the Tate Britain in 2014.
The artist remains a titan of American art.
But even before the virus some bodies were trying to stop the artist. Even in the past, long-haired weeping siren woman bodies would go to his exhibitions holding icons of the body of Ana Mendieta and they would cry and their eye salt would build up thick sediment crustacean skins on the brushed concrete floor. In the future there is a woman called Sophia and she is made of water.

Sophia slipped into the tear ducts of the screeching wet birdwomen and flowed out onto the floor of one of the last remaining fortified white cubes. She flowed and flowed until the gallery was overflowing with water and the water was more than wet, was filled with the tiny plankton and glowing fishes and the water itself (like the virus) might even be said to be alive. Sophia poured and flooded and twisted herself through the gallery, breaking its glass and she carried the titan on her back, squealing into his new iPhone. Screaming into the night.

Meanwhile the sirens flew off on their wings, with their sharpened beaks, to go and fuck all the art critics left who ignore them, to join the tormenting chorus. While some stayed in the water and grew scales and swam out to the sea where they gnashed their tails and their teeth and they lived without the gaping signifier of cunts and bit into the fibre optic cables; and infected the internet; what was left of her.

COLLAPSE

The punishment imposed by Mezentius on the soldiers of Aneas should be inflicted, by coupling him to one of his own corpses and parading him through the streets until his carcass and its companion were amalgamated by putrefaction.

A living Carl Andre was tied to the newly rotting corpse of Ana Mendieta with royal blue twine, face to face, mouth to mouth, limb to limb, with an obsessive exactitude in which each piece of the body corresponded with its matching putrefying counterpart. Shackled to this rotting double, the artist was left to decay. To avoid the starvation of Carl Andre - which would have been too much in keeping with his Minimalist refusal of excess - and to ensure the rotting bonds between living and dead artist were established, we continued to feed Carl Andre appropriately. Only once the superficial corporeal difference between the corpse and the living body started to rot away through the agency of maggots, which bridged the two bodies, establishing a differential continuity between them, did we stop feeding Carl Andre. Once the living man and the dead woman had turned black through putrefaction, we unshackled the bodies, now combined together through the digestion of worms, merged into black slime.

Both bodies shuddered with the lives of the maggots as we paraded them through our alleyways, trembled with the virus made flesh-eating. So we waited for Virus to take hold of their hearts – to start Ana's beating again as Carl Andre's throbbing organ burst through his skin and a million buzzing black flies swarmed out of the tattered shreds of flaccid flesh that was once his invisible masterbody.

And through his annihilation, Ana came back to life, preserving the other's difference from oneself.

Untitled, 1958, a poem by Carl Andre:

The ways of love were
sometime my revenge when
I was wronged by something
done or said & she stood
naked by the window waiting
to be struck perhaps where
her white breasts were

red...

A SPELL TO BIND MALE ARTISTS FROM MURDERING YOU

This spell should be used if you fear (like Ana Mendieta did, correctly, before she died) that a male artist is going to kill you

YOU WILL NEED:

A lump of clay/block of wood/paper/cloth etc. (any kind of sculptural or craft material)

Smokey quartz

Amethyst

Rosemary

Sage

Moss

Earth (preferably grave dirt)

An image of the artist's work or of their signature, either printed out or on a memory stick

Black ribbon/thread

This spell should be performed on a waxing or a full moon

**

Note: This spell is for protection only. Magic should not be used to harm the murderous male artist as any harm cast upon them will come back to the caster. (Instead we will chase him down together and he will be destroyed by our hands and teeth and skins and by the virus).

Representational magic (poppet magic/voodoo doll magic) is very strong and very dangerous because all representation is violence, so this spell should be performed very carefully. I also prefer to make poppets of artists' work instead of their bodies – this is also generally much simpler, especially with modern Masters, and can be done in a hurry. In an emergency (like when Ana Mendieta called her friend to say she was scared of Carl Andre, before he murdered her) you can even just draw an image of the artist's work with coloured pencil on paper.

Sew/sculpt/patch together a hollow poppet of the male artist's most famous work, but do not seal it up. If you cannot do the ritual right away store the doll in a piece of white cloth. Fill the poppet with earth (grave dirt if you can find it), rosemary, sage, a piece of smokey quartz, some moss and a piece of amethyst. During the ritual you will cleanse and consecrate the poppet as a way to finally link the male artist's body and career to their art-work. To seal this you should say:

Though separate you were,
Now you are one
The link of unison has now begun.

Sew or seal the poppet closed and the bind it mummy style. Bury the poppet after you have completed the ritual.

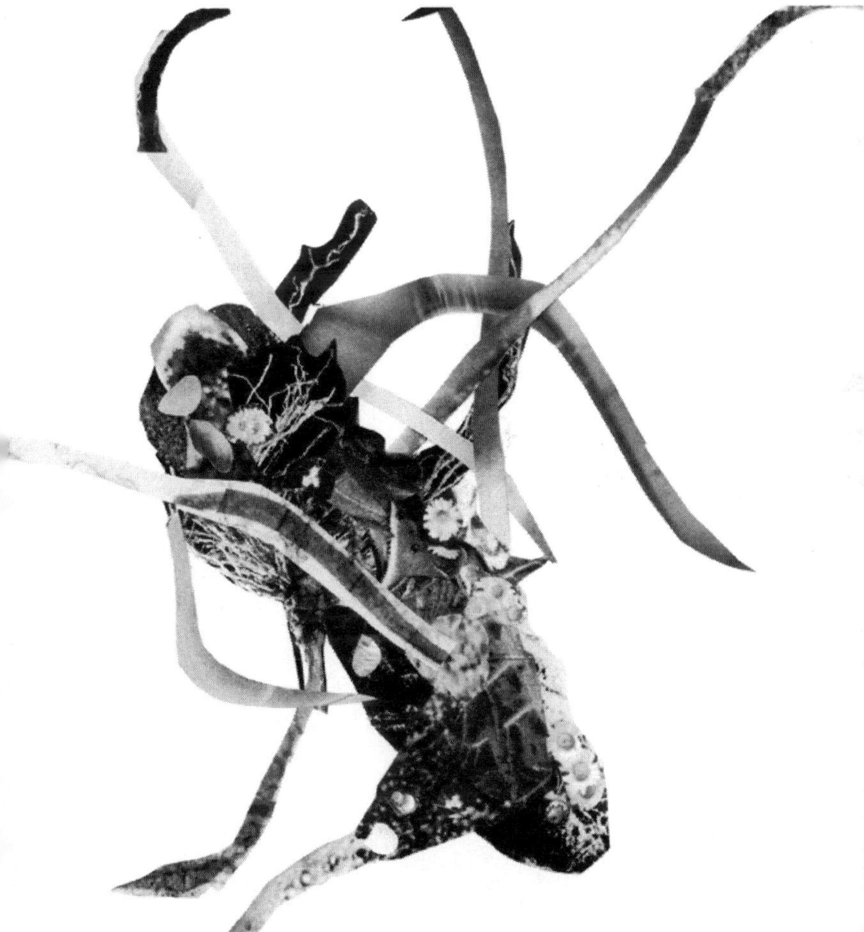

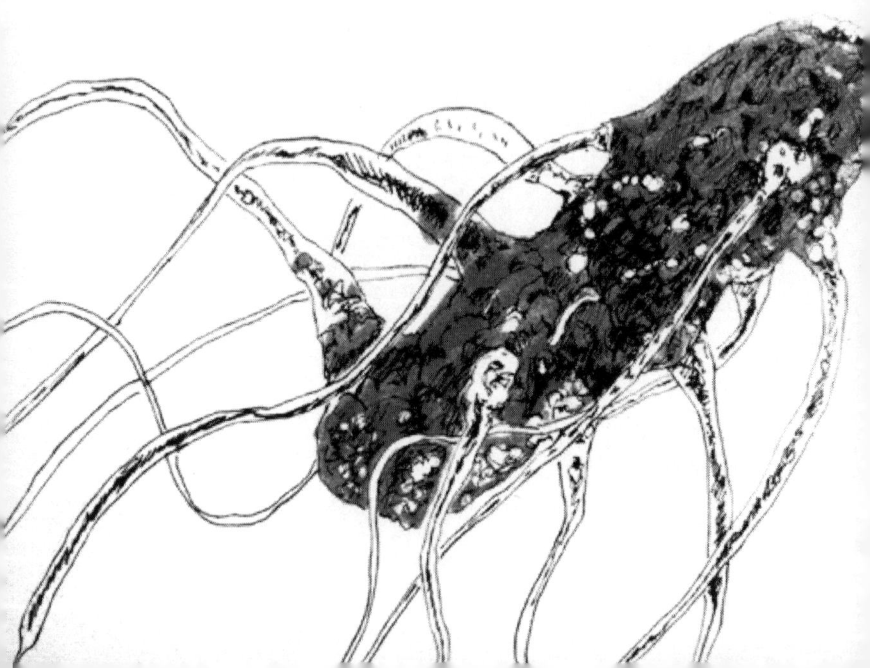

A SIGIL TO BIND MURDEROUS ART COLLECTORS AND GALLERISTS

A sigil is an unreadable representation; a symbol with magical significance, which is invisible to the reader (unless you are using a common recognised sigil such as for health or riches, and the reader is also a magic practitioner!). Sigils are also a type of representational magic and can be very powerful, although less dangerous than poppet magic. Sigils can also be extremely useful if you need to cast a spell that cannot be read, because you are expressing something that cannot be said in the space you are in.

YOU WILL NEED:

Any kind of image-making apparatus: paper and pen/pencil/marker/paint or Paint software/Photoshop/etc.

HOW TO MAKE A SIGIL

1. CREATE A STATEMENT OF INTENT

First, write down your desire very clearly, like this:

I WANT THE ZABLUDOWICZS TO LEAVE THE ART-WORLD ALONE AND LOSE ALL THEIR MONEY SO THEY CANNOT CONTINUE TO SUPPORT THE MURDER OF PALESTINIANS VIA ARMS/REAL ESTATE

Scan the letters and cross out any repeating ones, starting at the beginning of the sentence, as such:

I WANT ~~T~~HE ZABLUDO~~WI~~C~~Z~~S ~~TO LEAVE THE ARTWORLD~~ ~~ALONE AND LOSE ALL~~ ~~THEIR~~ M~~ONE~~Y ~~SO THEY CANNOT~~ ~~CONTINUE TO SUPPORT THE MURDER O~~F P~~ALESTINIANS~~ VI~~A ARMS/REAL ESTATE~~

Which leaves us with the following letters remaining:

IWANTHEZBLUDOCSYFPVRM

2. TURN YOUR STATEMENT OF INTENT INTO A MAGICAL SIGIL

On your piece of paper, or in your picture editing program make a basic, rough sketch linking the various letter shapes together, combining some of them as you go along (for example, an "M" is a "W" upside down, "I" is contained in "T", "F" is part of "E", "P" sits snugly in "B", etc.) What you're aiming for is a design that can be easily recalled by short term-memory, but not by long-term memory – you'll want to forget about the sigil. So too much simplicity is not a good thing. Easy enough to visualise in the ritual, easy enough to forget later on – that's the key to a good sigil.

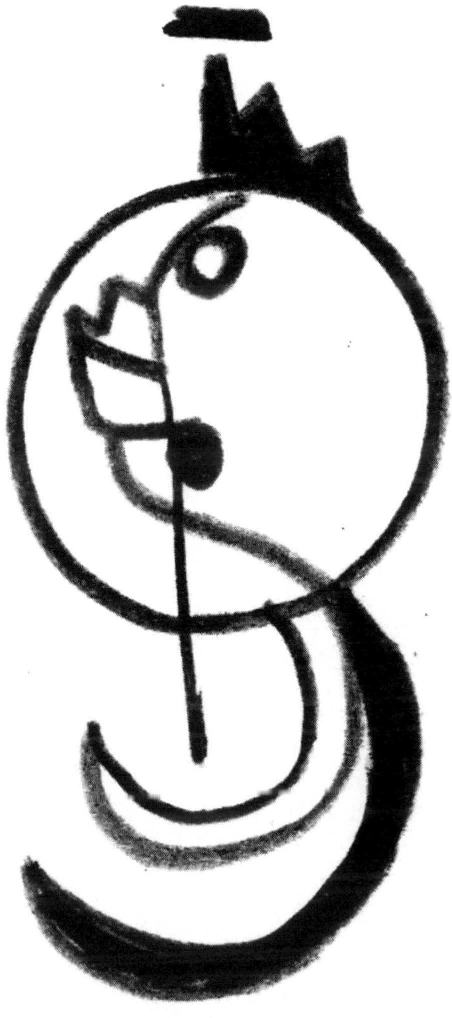

3. CHARM YOUR SIGIL

There are three ways you can charm your sigil:

Meditation

Look on your sigil and engage in a meditation, of at least fifteen minutes in which you focus on the sigil becoming a burning white light – focus on the image of the sigil burning, until eventually it burns out into nothingness.

Masturbation

Masturbate while visualising the sigil in your mind's eye, just the image, not the intent. At the point of orgasm, visualise the sigil becoming big and bright and then exploding/disintegrating into nothingness.

Dancing.

If you don't like masturbating but do like dancing and are able to, put on your favourite music and pour yourself into dancing – whatever that might mean to you (it might be swirling around or blinking or waving your hands). You just have to get to a point where you feel full of adrenalin and power and tingly and aren't really thinking anything. Then visualise the sigil in your mind's, eye, see it becoming big and bright.

Then stop dancing.

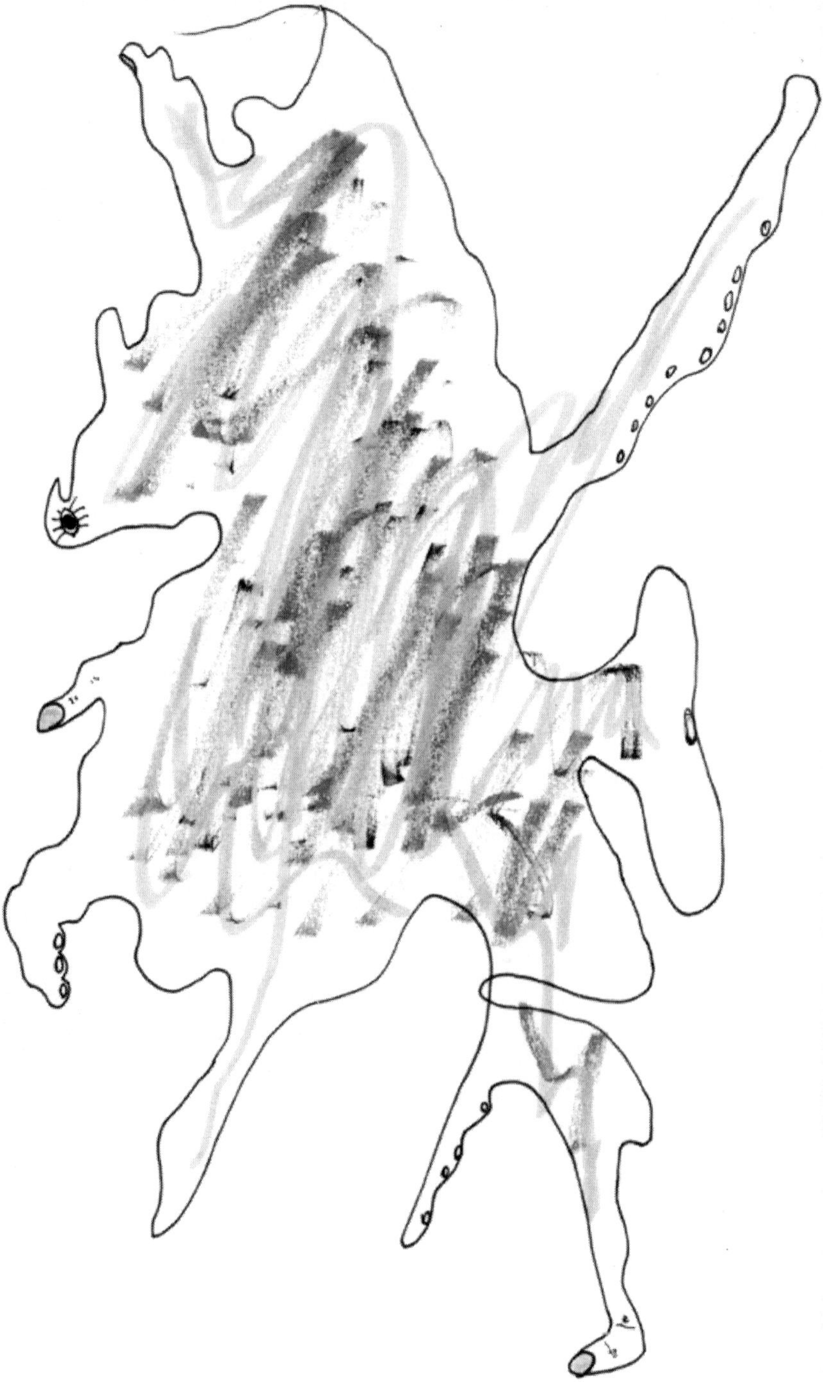

I want to show you a body. They are sitting on a rock and the rock is covered in moss grown out of the soil fertilised by the exploded skin of their enemies and their myopic futures. They are sitting on a rock and the moss is growing up into their arms and legs and heads: into their skin. There is a body and they are sitting on a rock and their eyes and lungs and spores and heads are shimmering all around towards the assembly of bodies around and inside of them. There is a body and they are sitting on a rock and the rock is covered in moss and the moss is spreading between their hot thighs and caressing their hot keys and

CHORUS: *(swallows and is swallowed by the body and the virus)*

THE END

Events and words taken from:

Tom Sparrow: The Plastic Subject of Alphonso Lingis. (2007)

Alphonso Lingis: Trust (2004)

Virus (1999 film)

Alphonso Lingis: Abuses (1994)

Robert Katz: Naked by the Window: The Fatal Marriage of Carl Andre and Ana Mendieta (1990)

Christine Redfern: Who is Ana Mendieta (2011)

Zombie Strippers (2008 film)

Ana Mendieta's Diary (20 March 1981)

Peter Shaffer: Equus (1973)

'Killswitch', the 11th episode of the 5th season of X Files, written by William Gibson and Tom Maddox (1998)

Will Crimson: Tentacle does the Twilight Zone (February 3, 2013)

Joseph Kosuth's Wikipedia Page.

http://sapiensanonym.blogspot.co.uk/

Joseph Conrad: Heart of Darkness (1899)

Julia Kristeva: Powers of Horror (1980)

Kathy Acker: Kathy Goes to Haiti (1990)

McKenzie Wark: A Hacker Manifesto (2004)

Kathy Acker: Against Ordinary Language: the Language of the Body (1997)

Ana Mendieta: Alma Silueta en Fuego (Silueta de Cenizas) (1975)

Valerie Walkerdine and Peter Bansel: Neoliberalism, work and subjectivity: towards a more complex account (2010)

Reza Negarestani: The Corpse Bride: Thinking with *Nigredo* (2008)

Shulamith Firestone: The Dialectic of Sex: The case for Feminist Revolution (1970)

Tom Dillon

My own experiences and fantasies

MANIFESTO!

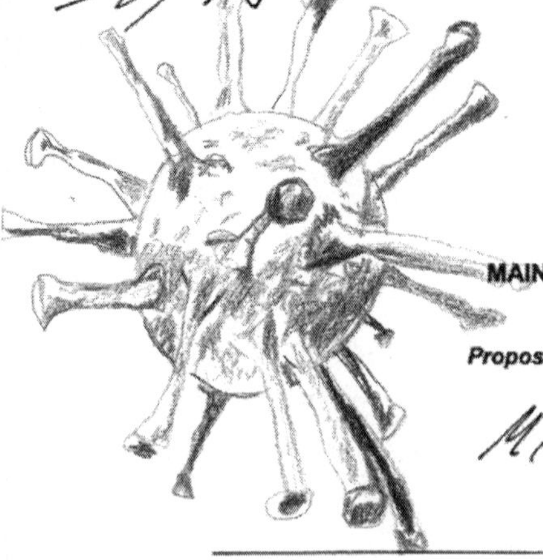

MAINTENANCE ART

Proposal for an exhibition "CARE"

MIERLE LADERMAN UKELES
© 1969

I. IDEAS

A. The Death Instinct and the Life Instinct:

The Death Instinct: separation; individuality; Avant-Garde par excellence; to follow one's own path to death—do your own thing; dynamic change.

The Life Instinct: unification; the eternal return; the perpetuation and MAINTENANCE of the species; survival systems and operations; equilibrium.

B. Two basic systems: Development and Maintenance. The sourball of every revolution: after the revolution, who's going to pick up the garbage on Monday morning?

Development: pure individual creation; the new; change; progress; advance; excitement; flight or fleeing.

Maintenance: keep the dust off the pure individual creation; preserve the new; sustain the change; protect progress; defend and prolong the advance; renew the excitement; repeat the flight;

show your work—show it again
keep the contemporaryartmuseum groovy
keep the home fires burning

Development systems are partial feedback systems with major room for change.
Maintenance systems are direct feedback systems with little room for alteration.

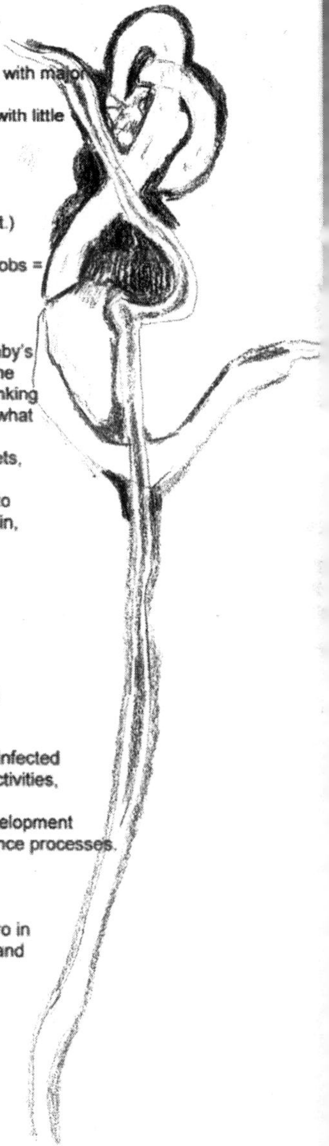

C. Maintenance is a drag; it takes all the fucking time (lit.)
The mind boggles and chafes at the boredom.
The culture confers lousy status on maintenance jobs = minimum wages, housewives = no pay.

clean you desk, wash the dishes, clean the floor, wash your clothes, wash your toes, change the baby's diaper, finish the report, correct the typos, mend the fence, keep the customer happy, throw out the stinking garbage, watch out don't put things in your nose, what shall I wear, I have no sox, pay your bills, don't litter, save string, wash your hair, change the sheets, go to the store, I'm out of perfume, say it again—he doesn't understand, seal it again—it leaks, go to work, this art is dusty, clear the table, call him again, flush the toilet, stay young.

D. Art:

Everything I say is Art is Art. Everything I do is Art is Art. "We have no Art, we try to do everything well." (Balinese saying).

Avant-garde art, which claims utter development, is infected by strains of maintenance ideas, maintenance activities, and maintenance materials.
Conceptual & Process art, especially, claim pure development and change, yet employ almost purely maintenance processes.

E. The exhibition of Maintenance Art, "CARE," would zero in on pure maintenance, exhibit it as contemporary art, and yield, by utter opposition, clarity of issues.

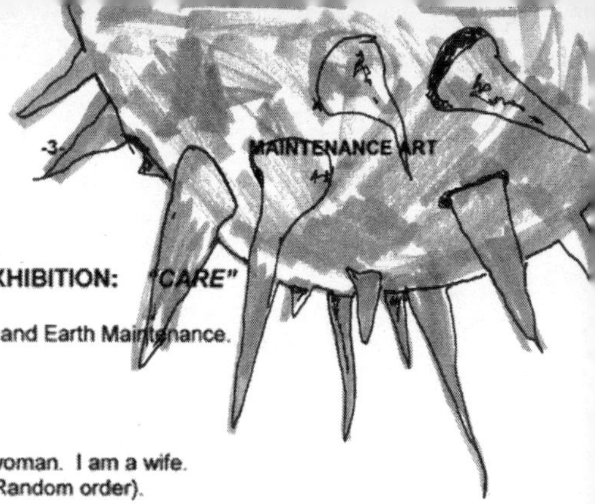

II. THE MAINTENANCE ART EXHIBITION: "CARE"

Three parts: Personal, General, and Earth Maintenance.

A. *Part One: Personal*

I am an artist. I am a woman. I am a wife.
I am a mother. (Random order).

I do a hell of a lot of washing, cleaning, cooking, renewing, supporting, preserving, etc. Also, (up to now separately I "do" Art.

Now, I will simply do these maintenance everyday things, and flush them up to consciousness, exhibit them, as Art. I will live in the museum and I customarily do at home with my husband and my baby, for the duration of the exhibition. (Right? or if you don't want me around at night I would come in every day) and do all these things as public Art activities: I will sweep and wax the floors, dust everything, wash the walls (i.e. "floor paintings, dust works, soap-sculpture, wall-paintings") cook, invite people to eat, make agglomerations and dispositions of all functional refuse.

The exhibition area might look "empty" of art, but it will be maintained in full public view.

MY WORKING WILL BE THE WORK

B. *Part Two: General*

Everyone does a hell of a lot of noodling maintenance work. The general part of the exhibition would consist of interviews of two kinds.

1. Previous individual interviews, typed and exhibited.

   Interviewees come from, say, 50 different classes and kinds of occupations that run a gamut from maintenance "man," maid, sanitation "man," mail "man," union "man," construction worker, librarian, grocerystore "man," nurse, doctor, teacher, museum director, baseball player, sales"man," child, criminal, bank president, mayor, moviestar, artist, etc., about:"

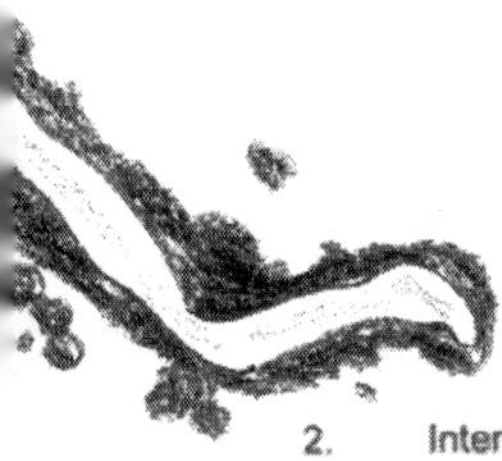

-what you think maintenance is;
-how you feel about spending whatever parts of your life you spend on maintenance activities;
-what is the relationship between maintenance and freedom;
-what is the relationship between maintenance and life's dreams.

2. Interview Room—for spectators at the Exhibition:

A room of desks and chairs where professional (?) interviewers will interview the spectators at the exhibition along same questions as typed interviews. The responses should be personal.

These interviews are taped and replayed throughout the exhibition area.

C. *Part Three: Earth Maintenance*

Everyday, containers of the following kinds of refuse will be delivered to the Museum:

-the contents of one sanitation truck;

-a container of polluted air;

-a container of polluted Hudson River;

-a container of ravaged land.

Once at the exhibition, each container will be serviced:

purified, de-polluted, rehabilitated, recycled, and conserved

by various technical (and / or pseudo-technical) procedures either by myself or scientists.

These servicing procedures are repeated throughout the duration of the exhibition.